EMBRACED

BY THE

CROSS

EMBRACED

BY THE

CROSS

DISCOVERING

THE PRINCIPLES

OF CHRISTIAN

FAITH AND LIFE

L.E. MAXWELL

MOODY PRESS
CHICAGO

© 2002 by
MOODY BIBLE INSTITUTE

Originally published as
Born Crucified © 1945

Library of Congress Cataloging-in-Publication Data

Maxwell, L.E.
    [Born crucified]
    Embraced by the Cross / L.E. Maxwell
        p. cm.
    Originally published: 1945.
    ISBN 0-8024-1137-1
    1. Sanctification. 2. Atonement. I. Title.

 BT765 .M37 2002
 232'.3--dc21

                                          2001054647

1 3 5 7 9 10 8 6 4 2

Printed in the United States of America

Contents

Preface

It was the French preacher Lacordaire who said that the church was "born crucified." By this he meant that all the members of the divine Head died *in* and *with* the last Adam, when He laid down His life on Calvary. As those who are born again to die, we must realize we are embraced by the Cross. These pages are an attempt in a small way to set forth, not as an exposition or theological statement, but in simple sermon and exhortation, the role of the Cross in the life of the believer.

Those who read these pages may conclude, before they have gone far, that the writer "seems spoiled for everything but to see people die." We are guilty, verily guilty. Dare we misapply Scripture to say, "Blessed are the dead who die in the Lord"? Resurrections follow such blessed deaths to self, even as day follows night.

A missionary from Africa recently said to us: "If only all of our missionaries had this teaching, it would be the solution of many of our difficulties on the field." Even so. The Cross is the key to all situations as well as to all Scripture. If I lose that key, I miss the road not only in the Bible, but also in the whole of my life. If, through the years, the Cross in the life of the believer had been adhered to as strenuously as the Cross for salvation, the church would not today be so plagued with modernistic infidelity. We little dream how we are suffering from what has been termed "a decapitated gospel." This book is written to show the believer that, from the moment he is saved, he is so related to the Cross, that, if he henceforth fails to live by the Cross, he is an utter ethical contradiction to himself and to his position in Christ.

Many of these chapters have been prepared too hurriedly and under tremendous pressure. Our prayer, therefore, is continually going up to the throne that in spite of our frailties and weaknesses in presentation, God may be glorified in all things through Jesus Christ, to whom be glory forever and ever.

Acknowledgments

First, the writer is especially indebted to Philip E. Howard Jr., editor of the *Sunday School Times*, who first proposed the writing of a series of articles for that valued paper on "The Cross in the Life of the Believer." This request was taken by the author as a call from God to prepare in book form the teachings herein set forth. Mr. Howard had granted very gracious permission that the chapters which appeared in the *Sunday School Times* be reprinted in this manner.

The writer acknowledges the great kindness of various authors and publishers, who have granted permission to use extracts from their copyrighted publications. Among these are the Society for Promoting Christian Knowledge, for selections from the books of Miss Amy Carmichael; Christian Publications, Inc., for selections from *The Way of the Cross*, by J. Gregory Mantle; Zondervan Publishing House and Marshall, Morgan and Scott, Ltd., for excerpts from the writings of F. J. Huegel, Dr. Ernest Gordon, and Dr. Samuel Zwemer; Moody Press for selections from *The Two-Fold Life*, by Dr. A. J. Gordon, and *Romans*, by William R. Newell; the China Inland Mission for a selection from *The Growth of a Soul*; Harper Brothers for a selection from *The Progress of Worldwide Missions*, by Dr. R. H. Glover.

We are also deeply indebted for brief quotations from the writings of various great saints such as Madame Guyon, Gerhard Ter Steegen, Charles Simeon, William Law, Andrew Murray, Bishop Moule, Mrs. Penn-Lewis, Oswald Chambers, and others. So familiar have we become with the writings of some of the leaders in the deeper truths of the Spirit that we find ourselves quoting them verbatim.

ONE

The Believer's Identification

During the Civil War, George Wyatt was drawn by lot to go to the front. He had a wife and six children. A young man named Richard Pratt offered to go in his stead. He was accepted and joined the ranks, bearing the name and number of George Wyatt. Before long Pratt was killed in action.

The authorities later sought again to draft George Wyatt into service. He protested, entering the plea that he had died in the person of Pratt. He insisted that the authorities consult their own records as to the fact of his having died in identification with Pratt, his substitute. Wyatt was thereby exempted as beyond the claims of law and further service. *He had died in the person of his representative.*

There we have the truth of identification in a nutshell. God's way of deliverance is through death nrough identification with our Substitute in His eath and resurrection.

After setting forth the truth of our justification through faith in Christ's death for us (in Romans 5), the apostle Paul sets forth at once (in Romans 6) the believer's identification with death. In chapter 5 it is Christ's death *for us;* in chapter 6 it is *our death with Christ.* Christ's death for us in chapter 5 is foundational and essential, but we should move on immediately into the next chapter. It is in chapter 6 we learn that our justification is no mere formal or legal transaction (although it is essentially a legal matter), but that it is also in essential union with Christ.

When God declares the ungodly sinner just, He makes no mere legal and lifeless imputation of righteousness apart from a real and deep life-union of the believer with Christ. God has indeed declared righteous "the ungodly," but not *apart* from Christ, not *outside* of Christ. We are justified only in Christ; that is, having come into vital life-union with Christ through faith in His atoning death. Those whom God declares righteous are "created in Christ Jesus." We are actually new creatures "in Christ."

After Paul's declaration in Romans 5:20 that "where sin abounded, grace abounded much more," the question naturally arises in Romans 6:1, "Shall we continue in sin that grace may abound?" The emphatic "Certainly not!" is based upon our identification with Christ in His death. Having been joined to Christ, it follows that we have been "baptized into His death" (6:3). Since we have been united to Christ crucified (in our justification—Romans 5), our position must be one of death "in Him." Paul says, "One died for all, then all died" (2 Corinthians 5:14). The death of Christ *for all* inevitably involved the death *of all*. We therefore died in Christ to sin. Shall we continue in sin? Perish the thought! "In sin" and "in Christ"? What an ethical contradiction!

Christ dying for me makes inevitable my death with Him. The very character of Christ's work on Calvary renders inseparable this double aspect of the once-for-all atonement. "Therefore what God has joined together, let not man separate." The cause of Christ suffers greatly today through what has rightly been termed a "dissected Cross, a decapitated gospel."

In taking upon Himself my "likeness of sinful flesh" (Romans 8:3), apart from which Christ could not have borne the penalty for my sin, He took me up into Himself—*made me one with Himself*. I am legally and ethically involved; I have been sentenced to death in Christ. It is my *judicial* position. Think a moment. Did I not accept death in order to be saved? When I realized I was death-doomed, I trusted the death of Another. Christ's death *for* sin is automatically my death *to* sin. God's way of victory and deliverance is to cut us right off from the old Adamic tree and to graft us into Christ, joining us to Him in death.

Apart, then, from any choice of my own, as a believer "I am crucified with Christ." My being a Christian makes inevitable a crucified life. It is the Christian life—not the deeper spiritual life. As an old theologian puts it, I have been "born crucified" (that is, when I was born again).

Has the reader labored and agonized to please God? You have resolved to read your Bible, to be more meditative and prayerful—all without effect.

You are conscious of crushing failure and defeat. In spite of all your effort, you are not like the Lord Jesus. The commands of Christ seem grievous. They come with no glad welcome. They haunt you. You are conscious that your life is an utter contradiction of the standards erected by the Lord Jesus as the normal Christian life. You may actually have wondered why the Savior made such demands. They only tantalize and torture you. And no matter how deeply you are shamed, pained, and repentant, your struggles avail you nothing.

Christ's requirements are indeed unattainables—*that* you must learn first of all. In His demands Christ goes far beyond the natural. He asks for no mere imitations. On the one hand He well knows your incapacities; on the other hand He demands the utterly impossible. And the necessary shock that has to come to the believer is that Christ's standards are completely beyond the reach of the flesh. Who naturally loves his enemies, rejoices in persecution, hates himself, and goes the second mile? Yet these things are native to the true Christian life.

We are at once indicted and hopeless. There is an impassable gulf between the humanly possible and the requirements of Christ. The flesh profits nothing. F. J. Huegel, in *Bone of His Bone*, rightly summarizes our failure thus: "We have been proceeding upon a false basis. We have conceived of the Christian life as an imitation of Christ. It is not an imitation of Christ. It is a participation of Christ."

Indeed we are to be partakers of the divine nature; and the doorway into such an experimental participation of the life of Christ is through identification—identification with Christ in His death and resurrection.

George Wyatt did not find deliverance by fighting the law or endeavoring to please the authorities. He took his death-position according to the government record. He acted on the basis of "It is written." He had died in the person of his representative. Even so, I, too, have a Substitute and Representative. He entered a deadly combat and died my death. I have been "crucified with Christ; it is no longer I who live, but Christ lives in me" (Galatians 2:20).

That is a great fact. No amount of struggling on my part can make it more true. I am an actual partaker of Christ, and, therefore, of His death and resurrection. Christ actually liveth in me. His is a life of death to sin and aliveness to God; it is mine to yield my all to Him—to believe and rejoice and rest *in Christ.*

An old missionary had long lived a defeated Christian life. In his despair his eyes fell upon the words, "Christ liveth in me" (KJV). "What," he said, "is Christ actually living in me?" He jumped up—solid Presbyterian though he was—and danced round and round his table, saying, "Christ liveth in me! Christ liveth in me!" When he realized that he was actually indwelt by the Crucified One, he came into blessed emancipation from the old self-life.

The life that is identified with Christ will be a life of sufficiency and fullness and victory. While it must not be confused with a life of emotion or of feelings, it is a life filled with "all joy and peace in believing." We must learn not to live in our feelings, for these are often misleading. The Lord Jesus said,

"You shall know the truth, and *the truth* shall make you free" (John 8:32; italics added).

The experience of a great pioneer of modern missions, J. Hudson Taylor, greatly illuminates this reality. After months of agony and struggle to realize more life, holiness, and power in his soul, he came in final and utter self-despair to "rest upon the Faithful One." In a letter to his sister he said in part:

> The sweetest part, if one may speak of one part being more sweet than another, is the *rest* which full identification with Christ brings. I am no longer anxious about anything . . . for He, I know, is able to carry out His will and His will is mine. It makes no matter where He places me or how. That is rather for Him to consider than for me. For the easiest positions He must give me grace, and in the most difficult, His grace is sufficient. So, if God places me in great perplexity, must He not give me much guidance; in positions of great difficulty, much grace; in circumstances of great pressure and trial, much strength? . . . As to work, mine was never so plentiful, so responsible, or so difficult; but the weight and strain are all *gone*. His resources are mine, for He is mine . . . *all this springs from the believer's oneness with Christ.*

> *Though I be nothing! I accept*
> *The uttermost Thou givest,*
> *One life alone between us now;*
> *One life—the life Thou livest.*
> *—Lucy A. Bennett*

The Secret
of Victory
Over Sin

During wartime, a man reported to his commanding officer, "I have taken a prisoner."

"Bring him along with you," his commander said.

"He won't come," complained the soldier.

"Well, then, come yourself," replied the officer.

"I can't. He won't let me," was the final acknowledgment.

I fear a great deal of Christian victory is no deeper than that. All Christians have indeed been freed from the penalty of sin. But what about sin's power? Are we to camp forever around the truth of our justification, that "where sin abounded, grace abounded much more"? Were we justified that we might be legally safe, or that we might become morally and spiritually sound? Were we not declared righteous in Christ that we might be holy in life?

Most of God's children seem to have assumed

the position that, having been justified, it is quite optional whether or not we live unto ourselves. Our restless and uneasy consciences would often stir us up to heart conviction of our unholiness. But we have contented ourselves with our judicial standing in Christ. We have misused and abused the blessed truth that "if anyone sins, we have an Advocate with the Father, Jesus Christ the righteous" (1 John 2:1). Perhaps unconsciously to ourselves, we have settled down to an ordinary and defeated Christian life, a customary unholiness. When the Captain of our salvation looks to us to be more than conquerors, to triumph in every place and take captivity captive, we cannot bring our sinful lives into obedience. "Well, then, come yourself," cries our Captain. But indwelling sinful self "won't let me."

Some Christians have been scared by the fanatical extremes of perfectionism. Their fears are not without foundation. However, we commend to the reader the wise words of Dr. A. J. Gordon:

> Divine truth as revealed in Scripture seems often to lie between two extremes. If we regard the doctrine of sinless perfection as a heresy, we regard contentment with sinful imperfection as a greater heresy. And we gravely fear that many Christians make the apostle's words, "If we say that we have no sin, we deceive ourselves," the unconscious justification for a low standard of Christian living. It were almost better for one to overstate the possibilities of sanctification in his eager grasp after holiness than to understate them in his complacent satisfaction with a traditional unholiness. Certainly it is not an edifying

spectacle to see a Christian worldling throwing stones at a Christian perfectionist.

But what says the Scripture? "Shall we continue in sin that grace may abound? Certainly not!" (Romans 6:1–2).

Is the reader one of those souls who has discovered that, whereas you thought you had taken a prisoner captive, you find yourself a slave, a veritable victim of self and indwelling sin? Do you find yourself "double-minded . . . [and] unstable in all [your] ways" (James 1:8)? Maybe you cry with Paul: "The good that I will to do, I do not do; but the evil I will not to do, that I practice" (Romans 7:19). You have watched and prayed. You have struggled and fought, you have mourned and wept over the futility of your effort to live for Christ. You may have tried to pray all night, or to "pray through" in order to "get the blessing." How often you have been filled with disgust and shame and secret weeping over your inward wrongness! But in spite of all your agonizing and strivings, you find your resolutions only so many ropes of sand.

Self can never cast out self. You are becoming weaker and weaker in your struggle against sin. Even your faith seems to be fading out. When you "will to" take sin a prisoner, bring him along, lock him up, and let him have no liberty, you find that you are actually the captive. Sin and self are in virtual control of the entire sweep of your life. What inward tragedy and conflict and defeat! Oh, the folly and futility of self-effort!

But there is a redeeming feature. Faith is often

born in despair. To become exceeding sinful in our own eyes may bring us to Paul's heart-rending cry: "O wretched man that I am! Who will deliver me from this body of death?" (Romans 7:24).

What is the matter? Wherein is our trouble? We have proceeded on the wrong basis. We have missed God's way of victory over sin. James H. McConkey well says: "God lays His foundations deep. Victory over sin He lays in *the deeps of death*. The Holy Spirit begins His triumphant teaching of the believer's victory over sin by one terse, striking, graphic phrase, 'dead to sin.'" Notice in Romans 6 the Spirit's emphasis on this death to sin: "dead to sin" (v. 2); "died unto sin" (v. 10); "dead indeed unto sin" (v.11; all KJV).

In verse 10 we have the truth that Jesus Christ died not only for sins, but that "he *died unto sin*"(KJV; emphasis added). When He was "made sin," God exacted of Him sin's penalty to the full. That penalty was death. In death, sin's penalty and power were exhausted. Sin's power, as well as sin's claims, are no more. Hence we read "death no longer has dominion over him" (v. 9). Christ died unto sin. He now lives forever unto God beyond the touch and reach of sin.

Paul asks: "Shall we continue in sin that grace may abound? Certainly not! How shall we who died to sin live any longer in it? Or do you not know that as many of us as were baptized into Christ Jesus were baptized into His death?" (Romans 6:1–3). Note that Paul does not say we have actually died, neither is he saying we are literally "dead to sin." But Paul is saying that which is true of every believer, namely, that he is *dead to sin through his union with Christ.* Each and every believer has been baptized by the Spirit into Christ. "He that is joined unto the Lord is one spirit"—one with the Crucified.

When Christ took upon Himself my humanity, apart from which He could never have borne the penalty for my sins, He made me one with Himself. I am identified with Him. He not only died *for me,* but I died *with Him.* He took me with Himself into death, and His death was my death to sin. He took me through the Cross, down into the tomb, and out of the tomb on and beyond the reach of sin's dominion. This is *the great basic fact.* The Holy Spirit says to you and to me: Know that Christ took your place, fastened you to Himself (Himself being in your very humanity), and took you into death, and through death out into glorious resurrection and emancipation from sin's dominion.

Regardless of our feelings, we are to *reckon* on this great fact—of our union with Christ in death and resurrection. "Reckon yourselves to be dead indeed to sin, but alive to God in Christ Jesus" (Romans 6:11). Note that Paul does not say, reckon sin dead to you. God's way of victory over sin is not through the *suppression* of sinful desires, nor through the *eradication* of the old nature, nor yet through the *cleansing* of inbred sin. God's way of victory is through *crucifixion*—deliverance is only through *death.*

There is a vast difference between reckoning myself dead to sin and reckoning sin dead to me. Every attempt to make sin dead to me, through self-effort, or struggle, or blessing, or make-believe, is not following the scriptural pattern. God says I am to reckon myself dead to sin. If I am willing to be rid of sin, my faith should fasten on the fact of my death to sin through my actual life-union with Christ. I am "in Christ." And to be in Him is to be "dead to sin."

Oh, to believe it! Never mind the feelings. Each time I come up against some particular sin, let me there say: "I died to that in Christ." If it be a worldly attraction: "I am crucified to the world and the world unto me." If it be proud, haughty self, again let me reckon: "One died for all, all died." Then I should not, and need not, live unto myself—I am dead to my selfish pride and conceit and haughtiness.

It is said that Emperor William refused a request for an audience prepared by a German-American. The Emperor declared that Germans born in Germany but naturalized in America became Americans: "I know Americans; I know Germans; but German-Americans I do not know." Even so, I was once bound in Adam. I am now freed in Christ. The Cross cut me off, killed me outright to the old citizenship and life. I am no Adam-Christ believer. Such a position will get me no audience with my King, bring me no deliverance from bondage to the old man. Let me cease at once any such unholy duplicity. Let me declare that I am Christ's and His alone. Let me yield fully unto Him as one "dead indeed to sin, but alive to God in Christ Jesus our Lord."

THREE

The Cross
and Death
to Sin

I t means everything to me, as a Christian, that I was "born crucified," that is, born all over again through death—the death of Jesus Christ. When I was saved, I accepted death as my only deliverance. I had been embraced by the Cross.

Christ died in my place. I was indeed a dead man but for Christ. He died my death. "Who his own self bare our sins in his own body on the tree, that we, being dead to sins, should live unto righteousness" (1 Peter 2:24 KJV). I must be either "dead in sins" or "dead to sin." If I am lost in Adam, I am "dead *in* sins." If I am saved through union with Christ, I am "dead *to* sin." When I accepted Christ's death for my sin, I could not avoid accepting my own death to sin. Christ died, not only *for* sin, but *unto* sin. I am committed to the Cross. To attempt any other position is to involve myself in an infamous moral contradiction.

My only logical standing is one of death. I have been "born crucified"; I am embraced by the Cross. It is a first principle of the Christian life.

This is no mere mechanical thing, no mere legal fiction. I am actually and vitally joined to Christ. But, like every other Bible truth, it calls for my hearty consent. That Christ indeed "lives in me" is a glorious truth. If I am saved, that is no mere cold, lifeless imputation. It is a fact. But it is a truth that calls for my most cordial "Amen." That I may realize His indwelling, I am commanded to reckon myself dead unto sin but alive to God in Christ Jesus. Such reckoning is not make-believe or, as someone said, "Trying to make yourself believe what isn't so." However, the reckoning of a lively faith implies more than is usually realized.

Reckoning, in order to be real, includes *self-renunciation*. Our reckoning is doomed to failure unless we renounce self. In the power of Christ's death I must refuse my old life. On the basis of Calvary and of my oneness with Christ in His death, I must refuse to let self lord it over me. I must choose whether I will be dominated by the hideous monster self or by Christ. The life that "Christ lives in me" must have a happy "yet not I" at its very heart. How can I have the benefits of Christ's death while I still want my own way? Self must be dethroned. I am indeed promised newness of life, but only on the basis that I put off the old. If Christ went into the abysmal depths of self-emptying and self-renunciation, I must sink my old self-life into harmony with His ignominious departure. Let me with Samuel Rutherford "put my hand to the pen and let the Cross of the Lord Jesus have my submissive and resolute Amen."

When we thus begin to renounce self, we shall find that this will generally be done through our submission to someone in the family or business circle. Home missions are good; foreign missions are better; but "submissions" at home and abroad are best of all. There are some women who will find practical victory at home through submitting to that husband's temper; some men through accepting the lashes of that long-tongued wife; others through embracing that seeming handicap or infirmity. Often we can believe for victory only around some such practical obedience. In each case self is renounced. Reckoning without the practical renunciation of self proves mere make-believe. It is just more self-righteousness, more self-effort.

Reckoning also includes *rejection of sin*. Paul says: "Reckon yourselves to be dead indeed to sin," and then adds, "Do not let sin reign." We should not let sin reign. That we already know. But better still, we need not let sin reign since we died and passed through death into resurrection beyond sin's dominion. Sin has no claim over those united to the Crucified One, and sin "shall not have dominion" over those who yield themselves entirely to the Holy Spirit. "For the law of the Spirit of life in Christ Jesus has made me free from the law of sin and death" (Romans 8:2). But as long as we have any controversy with the Holy Spirit, we cannot escape sin's dominion. The Spirit of God is specific and the Scripture is plain. The "offending" member is to be done to death —not pampered, or even prayed about. It is indeed good to pray for blessings, and to cry out for clean hearts, but not when God says "cut off" and "pluck out." God has truly cut us off from all evil at the Cross. He now says: It is yours to break with sin— "Therefore do not let sin reign" (Romans 6:12).

In order to have "a conscience void of offense toward God, and toward men," how long has it been since I had to humble myself and be "put . . . to an open shame" before my family, or my business friend, or my Sunday school class, or my congregation? Dare I say that I have offended none and that the Holy Spirit has not pleaded with me in some such connection to obey Him? Christ was willingly set at naught, willingly classed with criminals. He willingly died to rid me of sin. Let me, then, not pamper, but pour contempt on all my pride. Let me go at once and humble myself. If I will not take my sin to the place of shame, cost me what it may to get rid of it, how can I claim the cutting-off power of Calvary? I am out of harmony with the Cross. Confession of sin implies rejection of sin. Its power is broken only as we come into harmony with the Cross.

But the Cross is no place of concealment, of hiding, of covering sin. It is the place where we break with sin, the place of exposure, of guilt, of open shame. Let me be willing to lose face and abide by all the consequences. If Christ died to rid me of sin, should I not rather die than retain it? But if we are not yet sick enough of sin to be rid of sin, we can only bow, and bleed, and hug our chains, until we are "sick unto death" of sinful self. We must be driven out of our unholy duplicity and made to own our double-mindedness.

But God is good. Christ is a jealous lover. He wants every believer delivered. He will not shrink from reducing you to shame and despair if only you may be exposed to the power generated on your behalf at Calvary. You must learn by kindness or by terror. God's sword of providence may be laid successively to every tie that binds you to self and sin. Wealth and health and friends may fall before that sword. The inward fabric of your life will go to pieces. Your joy will depart.

Smitten within and without, burned and peeled and blasted, you may finally, amidst the dreadful baptism, be driven from the sinful inconsistency of living for yourself. You may at length be *disposed* (blessed word—sweet compulsion) to yield self over to the victory and undoing of Calvary. Oh, the glorious power of the Cross! How can we longer hold out against it? All the power generated at Calvary is at your disposal.

In *Bone of His Bone*, F. J. Huegel tells about the strange lot of certain young ladies employed in a laboratory where contact with radium is inevitable. Upon entering this factory, they know their fate is sealed. They will die. After a limited time they are released from their work with a handsome check for $10,000 [a major sum in the 1940s]. Doctors have examined girls who have thus toiled in contact with radium and have found by means of the X ray that a strange fire consuming the life burns in their bones. This most highly concentrated force is killing them. But a still more highly concentrated force was released at Calvary. There Heaven's radium was focused upon the great cancer of humanity's sin and shame. Radium kills. There is no power under heaven that can stand its concentrated dynamic. "The Cross kills," Huegel notes. "The man who exposes himself to Calvary soon discovers that a hidden fire burns within his bones."

Oh, let me, then, put no limit to its concentrated force. May its death-dealing, yea, life-giving and healing rays penetrate my most secret life, until its hidden fire burns in all the bones of my inmost being. Let the radium of the Crucified One be applied again and again. It is a process. But let me not fear to expose myself to the divine treatment. If I am indeed sick of shams and hollow-hearted pretense—if my heart is hot with a veritable "furnace of desire" for deliverance—if my soul thirsts for the wells of living water, the full-orbed message of Calvary will be welcomed with joy unspeakable and full of glory.

In all the gladness of Christ's glorious triumph let me say again and yet again: I have been and am crucified with *Christ*, it is no more I that live but Christ who lives in me—lives in me, even me—His own death-resurrection life, a life of death to sin and aliveness unto God.

Dying with Jesus,
By death reckoned mine;
Living with Jesus,
A new life divine.

FOUR

The Cross
and the
World

The Roman orator Cicero summarized the attitude of the ancient world to the Cross when he said: "Not only let the cross be absent from the person of Roman citizens, but its very name from their thoughts, eyes and ears." Two thousand years ago we find no halo of glory, no beautiful associations of history, no nobility, and no thought of heroic sacrifice attached to the Cross.

How cluttered up is the Cross at the present time! As soon as the Cross ceases to be to us, first of all, the place of utmost shame and contempt, we make the Cross of Christ of no effect.

In Christ's day the disciples must often have beheld the procession of criminals, murderers, and rebels carrying their crosses on their way to an ignominious departure—a death of such infamy and shame and execration that we have no word that is significant of the deep and universal detestation that belonged to the cross in early times. Add to all this the scriptural anathema and capstone "He who is hanged is accursed of God" (Deuteronomy 21:23), and we begin to understand the offense (literally, the scandal) of the Cross.

Yet it was only in the Cross that the princes of this world could find an adequate expression of their unrelenting and venomous hatred of the Christ of God. There, once and for all, the proud world spoke its mind out loud. The Cross, then, perfectly photographs the world's thought of Christ. "They all cried out at once, saying, 'Away with this Man. . . . Crucify Him, crucify Him!'" (Luke 23:18, 21). Be not deceived, my friend, that dagger is still there, albeit hidden in the world's skirts. It is still true that the "one pulse by which we can measure the real spirituality of an epoch, or of a soul, or of a group of souls, is the measure of horror they find in the word 'world'" (D. M. Panton).

It is not easy to define the word *world*. The Scriptures speak of "the ruler of this world" (John 12:31); of "the course of this world" (Ephesians 2:2) which is according to "the god of this world" (2 Corinthians 4:4 KJV); of "the spirit of the world," which is contrary to the Spirit of God (1 Corinthians 2:12); of "the form of this world," which is passing away (1 Corinthians 7:31); and of the wisdom of this world, which "crucified the Lord of glory" (1 Corinthians 2:8).

Little wonder, then, that God says: "Do not love the world"—the whole orbit and life of the natural man—"or the things in the world" (1 John 2:15).

This last clause is important. It is likely that many of my readers are, as a whole, unworldly. But let me ask, Are you the victim of a single worldliness? To what thing are you passionately attached? You may rightly condemn the teenager's love of the dance, the show, the theater. But are you under the spell of politics, or art, or science, or money, or ambition, or social popularity, or business power? The world is a different world to a young person than it is to the middle-aged or older person. But the narcotic is no less deadly. Since the world slew Christ, and hates God, its whole ambition and passion and swagger, its popularity and pleasure—yea, its ten thousand enchantments—all contradict the Cross and exclude "the love of the Father." The apostle does not say, "Love it not too much, or love it not so much"; he simply says, "Love it not at all."

The apostle next defines the three chief roots of all worldliness, all so like the three golden apples that lured the legendary Atalanta to a lost race. "For all that is in the world—the lust of the flesh, the lust of the eyes, and the pride of life—is not of the Father, but is of the world" (1 John 2:16). Selfish man seeks satisfaction through these three forms of lust. But to all of them the Christian has been crucified. Let him not come down from the cross. "They that are Christ's have crucified the flesh with the affections and lusts" (Galatians 5:24 KJV). But, oh, the uncrucified lusts that are lording it over God's children and putting the Crucified One to an open shame!

However, the infinite cunning and craft of the world-spirit are beyond the natural mind to detect. It is an enchantment, a witchery, a pageantry vastly seductive. Worldly-mindedness in multiple form has thrust its cancerous roots into the very fiber of our religious life. It is a deadly leprosy, unaccompanied by pain, but eating to the bone. It is the white ant that has eaten away the frame of our spiritual house. It is the seed-bed of intellectualism, the handmaid of modernism. It is the fifth column boring from within, which has unseated and ousted the spirit of the Cross.

"Some of us read, years ago," says J. Gregory Mantle, "of a mountain of loadstone which drew by its tremendous power of attraction every piece of iron that was brought within the range of its influence. Ships at sea, passing near the shore of that land where the mountain was, felt its force on their anchors and chains and bars. At first their approach to the mountain was scarcely perceptible. There was a declining from their course which excited very little apprehension. But the attraction gradually became stronger, until, with ever increasing velocity, the vessel was drawn closer. Then the very bolts and nails started from the vessel's beams and planks, and fastened themselves on the sides of the mountain, the vessel, of course, falling to pieces and becoming a total wreck."

Let us then set forth a few subtle forms of worldliness which lure us to the rocks, and wreck our Christian testimony. Note:

- Our dread of the faces and frowns of worldly men. On the other hand, what a pleasant morsel is the world's favor and flattery!

- The unwarranted time we can spend over some trifling hobby instead of "redeeming the time." We call it relaxation, but there may be much worldliness in it.
- The ease with which we can sit in slippered feet noting the world's news when we might be giving the "good news" to lost men. We refuse to endure hardness as good soldiers of Jesus Christ. Our soft little "world" has us.
- The prevalent lust for late night lunching and vainglorious witticisms—cheating ourselves of the time needed for God's fellowship in the Word and prayer next morning. Then we go out ungirt and stripped of our armor to meet the world at large—all because of our own secret inner worldliness.
- The great place we give to likes, dislikes, and personal choices.

How much we are regulated by public opinion, perhaps religious opinion, rather than scriptural principle.

How easily we are content to allow this or that thing, be it ever so innocent or lovely, to becloud the world to come.

How little we count it a privilege to suffer shame for His name.

What expectations we have of great contentment and satisfaction from certain earthly comforts. How fond we are of nice things and luxuries, and how unwilling to forego them for the sake of sending the gospel to the heathen.

How we abhor being counted eccentric! How

unquestioningly obedient we are to fashion's de-
crees, not because the styles are reasonable or right
or decent, for they are often most unreasonable and
indecent. We are so worldly minded we would
rather be indecent than different. Old King Lust
calls thus: "Do this," and many do it as obediently as
any centurion's servant ever obeyed under the lash
of his Roman master.

Until we personally take ourselves in hand, we
need not wonder at the false doctrine, the modernistic ministry, the poor church discipline (or
none), and the corrupt practices in the church. The
whole root of our ruin is found in worldliness. As
William Law so well puts it: "The heresy of all here-
sies is a worldly spirit. Whence is all the degeneracy
of the present Christian church? I should place it all
in a worldly spirit."

FIVE

The Cross, Conflict, and Final Victory

I was once drowning in the world's depths and condemnation. But "He sent from above, He took me; He drew me out of many waters" (Psalm 18:16). How deep were the seas into which the Savior sank that He might "deliver [pluck out, rescue] us from this present evil world" (Galatians 1:4 KJV). How wonderful our rescue!

Further victory is needed, however, in getting *the sea taken out of us*. Yet it is crowning victory when those rescued plunge back into the sea to rescue other perishing ones. Even so. After the victory of being taken out of the world, and after the victory of having the foul elements of this world's darkness taken out of us, there is the crowning victory of getting us sent into that very world to rescue other perishing ones from the world's doom.

However, in reentering this present evil world, it

is imperative that our relationship to that world be kept crystal clear before us. Having been born from above, our citizenship is in heaven. We have been spiritually disfranchised of the world. Christ says plainly, "You are not of the world" (John 15:19). We have been crucified to the world and the world to us. And how great the moral distance between the crucified disciple and the crucified world? As far asunder as the throne of heaven is from the gate of hell, and as different in disposition as lambs in the midst of wolves. With what bold and daring contrast we are to stand out as sons of God in the midst of a crooked and perverse generation among whom we are to shine as lights in the world!

In John 17 Jesus sets forth the Christian's position as *taken out of* the world (v. 6), *not of* the world (v. 14), *kept from the evil of* the world (v. 15), *left in* the world (v. 11), *sent into* the world to *preach to* the world (vv. 18, 20), and as a result *hated by* the world (v. 14). Since our message centers around the world's attitude to the Cross, this last point is important.

Settle it in your mind, O Christian, that because you are not of the world, the world hates you. Minimize not the world's hatred of the truth. The world that crucified Christ will not be able to tolerate you. The worldlings will clash madly against you. The reproach of Christ will fall upon you from all quarters. Think it not strange. It is a mark of true discipleship: "All who desire to live godly in Christ Jesus will suffer persecution" (2 Timothy 3:12).

Let no one think that we write as one who has any morbid greed for persecution, or that we hold any brief for a self-made martyrdom. Perish all such contemptible hypocrisy! But, without contradiction, the only reason the scandal of the Cross has ceased for some professed disciples is that they have become so compromising that the world is no longer rebuked by their lives or testimony. The church and the world, like Samson and Delilah, are found in an unhallowed and foul fellowship.

And they of the Church, and they of the World,
Journeyed closely, hand and heart,
And none but the Master, who knoweth all,
Could discern the two apart.

One of the most searching and condemning sentences that ever fell from the Savior's lips was that uttered to His own unbelieving brethren: "The world cannot hate you" (John 7:7). If ever I become so one with the world, so tolerant of its spirit and atmosphere that I reprove it no more, incur not its hatred, rouse not its enmity to Christ—if the world can find in me no cause to hate me and cast me from its company—then I have betrayed Christ and crucified Him afresh in the house of His friends. On intimate terms with this world that nailed Him to the tree? Perish the thought!

When I am in full identification with Christ, the world can regard me as only fit for crucifixion. And as a disciple of Christ I should no more covet the favor of this crucified world than I would court and covet the smile of a cursed and crucified and expiring felon.

"It is the first condition of our initiation into the secret society of the Friends of God, that we take our place with Him before the judgment seat of the world; and are with Him mocked, patronized, and misunderstood by the world's religion, the world's culture, the world's power—all the artificial contrivances that it sets up as standards by which to condemn Reality," writes James Cordilier in *The Glory of the Cross.* "In the very moment in which we declare that it cannot give us that intangible Kingdom to which we aspire, we alienate its sympathy, insult its common sense. It goes up into the judgment seat, prepared to deal wisely with the rebel in us, tolerantly with the fool. Then ignorance, idleness, and cowardice condemn us at their ease."

One of the teachers of the past generation who had an unusually clear conception of the Christian's place in the world was Dr. A. I. Gordon. He once said:

The men who conquered the Roman Empire for Christ bore the aspect of invaders from another world, who absolutely refused to be naturalized to this world. Their conduct filled their heathen neighbors with the strangest perplexity; they were so careless of life, so careful of conscience, so prodigal of their own blood, so confident of the overcoming power of the blood of the Lamb, so unsubdued to the custom of the country in which they sojourned, so mindful of the manners of that country from whence they came not. The help of the world, the patronage of its rulers, the loan of its resources, the use of its methods they utterly refused, lest by employing these they might compromise their King. . . . But there can be no reasonable doubt that that age in which the church was so completely separated from the world was the age in which Christianity was most victorious in the world.

Professor H. B. Workman has summarized the Christian's lot under imperial Rome:

> For two hundred years to become a Christian meant the great renunciation, the joining a despised and persecuted sect, the swimming against the tide of popular prejudice, the coming under the ban of the Empire, the possibility at any moment of imprisonment and death under its most fearful forms. For two hundred years he that would follow Christ must count the cost, and be prepared to pay the same with his liberty and life. For two hundred years the mere profession of Christianity was itself a crime. . . . "Public hatred," writes Tertullian, "asks but one thing, and that not investigation into the crime charges, but simply the confession of the Christian name."

The Romans, Greeks, or other Gentiles were indifferently called "the first race." The Jews, admittedly different, were known as "the second race." But the Christians, so peculiarly "disfranchised of the world," so intolerant of the world's spirit and atmosphere, and standing out in such bold contrast and daring unworldliness, were stigmatized "the third race." The Christians willingly embraced the stigma. Anything was better than sin. Let the heathen rave. Christians belonged to another world. They were "dead to all the globe"—out of joint with all the world. Thus the cry in the circus of Carthage: "How long must we endure *this third race?*"

The results of such an uncompromising victorious testimony were inevitable. The church of today cannot endure the blaze kindled by those martyr fires. Such "burning and shining lights" discover to us how distant is our departure from the Crucified One. Mark well, O popular Christian and worldly-wise preacher, venturing how far you must go with the world in order to win the world: Never had the Church so much influence over the world as when she had nothing to do with the world. Completely separated from that Roman world, those early Christians plunged back into that sunken Empire to lift it off its hinges and change the entire course of the world's history. But in speaking of those early days, Tertullian wrote: "We engage in these conflicts as men whose very lives are not our own."

SIX

The Cross
and
Consecration

The author has a dear friend in the ministry who, as a young man, tried again and again to give himself fully to the Lord, but without success. He was perfectly sincere, but he continued perfectly miserable. He was one of those many young people who are continually consecrating themselves to the Lord.

At length he came to discover that he had missed the very basis of consecration. He found light through God's own "consecration" of the Old Testament priests. When he beheld the blood placed on the priest's ear, on his thumb, on his toe, and saw him sprinkled all over with blood, he came to understand his union with "Christ made sin." He saw death written all over him. He felt the awful doom and death to which Calvary committed him. He came to understand his identification with Christ.

He saw himself one with the Crucified in His death and resurrection. This death-life union changed his whole conception of surrender to Christ and laid the foundations in his life for a successful and abiding consecration.

Such an experience is not uncommon among Christians. They have been "justified by faith [and] have peace with God through our Lord Jesus Christ." But they have not realized the implications of the Cross. In some of our best churches they have been immediately taken from this justification of Romans 5:1 to the truth of consecration as set forth in Romans 12:1–2. We would not be overcritical in that which is well meant; but to ignore or pass over the teaching and amazing declarations of our union with Christ as set forth in Romans 6 to 8 is not really the proper approach to consecration.

Such a skirting of these underlying truths brought many years of misery to my ministerial friend. He knew not the way of victory over sinful self. All unconsciously he was attempting in the energy of self to lay his all on the altar. When he came to see that he was already the Lord's through his life-union with Christ—already crucified and risen with Christ, "dead indeed to sin, but alive to God in Christ Jesus our Lord" (Romans 6:11)—he then had a sure basis for presenting himself unto God. At last he had found the blessed secret of success. But let me further illustrate.

When Abraham Lincoln delivered his address at the dedication of the battlefield cemetery in Gettysburg, Pennsylvania, on November 19, 1863, he said:

We have come to dedicate a portion of that field as a final resting place for those who here gave their lives. . . . But, in a larger sense, we cannot dedicate—we cannot consecrate—we cannot hallow—this ground. The brave men, living and dead, who struggled here, have consecrated it far above our poor power to add or detract. . . . It is for us, the living, rather, to be dedicated here to the unfinished work . . . to be dedicated to the great task remaining before us.

We speak of Christian consecration. But, in a larger sense, we cannot dedicate—we cannot consecrate—we cannot hallow—this ground of our already redeemed lives. In His laid-down life, the Crucified One has already "consecrated it [us] far above our poor power to add or detract." Let us fix our eyes upon Christ. We have already been fastened to Christ Crucified. Let us believe that if we be dead with Him we shall also live with Him.

The blessed truths clustering around our death-resurrection union with Christ, as set forth in Romans 6–8, lay the basis for a successful consecration, as so clearly set forth in Romans 12:1–2. Having been so completely redeemed and "accepted in the Beloved," Christ now beseeches us by His own infinite and many tender mercies to present our bodies a reasonable, living, holy, acceptable sacrifice to Himself. As we lay our hands upon the sacred and holy head of our Burnt Offering, we know (let it be the language of a lively faith) that in Him we are a sweet savor unto God—a sweet savor of perfect obedience, perfect consecration, and perfect sacrifice "far above our poor power to add or detract."

What power! What persuasion! What perfect peace! His is the perfect satisfaction—a sweet savor offering made by fire—ours the sweet privilege of being burned out for Him.

Can we not trust Him? Shall we not let Him carry us where He will? O hesitating believer, are we not ready to sign away our rights and reserves for all coming days? Come. Give Him all. "It is more blessed to give than to receive" and "God loves a cheerful giver" (Acts 20:35; 2 Corinthians 9:7). Let us launch forth with Him on any uncharted sea. Those who sail the high seas in treacherous times commit themselves to His Majesty the King: "At your service, Sir, with sealed orders." It was George Whitefield who said: "I give up myself to be a martyr for Him who hung upon the Cross for me. I have thrown myself blindfolded and, I trust, without reserve into His almighty hands."

Miss Ahn, that heroic lady of Korea, had argued with God for some seven years against going to the Japanese Diet and warning that nation against persecuting the Christians for refusal to bow at the Shinto shrines. When she finally yielded to obey God's call, she sold all her possessions and bought a one-way ticket for Tokyo—to do and, if necessary, die. We say that consecration is "for service or sacrifice." To Miss Ahn it was both. Hers would be a trip to death. She bought that one-way ticket compelled by love to obey—to go, to do, and, yes, to die.

Oh, to be so sweetly constrained by Calvary's awful compulsion that we can hold out no longer, can no longer resist its attractive force! We are drawn to death—with appetites whetted to eat of the Great Sacrifice. Ah, this is life indeed, life more abundant, the life that is hid with Christ in God—"He who feeds on Me will live because of Me" (John 6:57).

But there is another aspect that is all important. Frances Ridley Havergal has said: "Full consecration may in one sense be the act of a moment and in another the work of a lifetime. It must be complete to be real, and yet, if real it is always incomplete; a point of rest, and yet a perpetual progression." Let us not be deceived, we shall often be compelled to say with the psalmist: "God is the Lord, and He has given us light [conversion]; bind the sacrifice with cords to the horns of the altar [consecration]" (Psalm 118:27). It will cost us all we have and all we are to keep in this consecrated mind.

We shall be forced to cry out again and again as we fear the fire and feel the sacrificial knife, "Bind me, blessed Savior, as a sacrifice—fasten me with Thy cords of constraining love lest I finish my course with shame. Let me not begin to make provision anywhere for the flesh—let my offering continue to be a burnt offering—a whole burnt offering, yea, a continual burnt offering. Let me never come down from the cross to save myself. Fix me, fasten me, bind me with Thine own cords to Calvary, a continual burnt offering."

A missionary friend returned to his field seeking a fresh anointing. He says: "The Lord searched my heart and my possessions to see if anything had become dearer to me than Himself. 'Lovest thou me more than these?'—meaning my wife and boy. I hesitated. I felt as though He had laid before me an execution warrant and was waiting for my signature. There was a terrible fight in my heart: surrender meant death. After a long struggle and by His grace, I made the surrender and I did it with the fullest expectation that this meant the end of their earthly lives. After a few weeks, while returning to our little Japanese house alone, the thought flashed into my mind, 'The boy is sick.' He was all right when I left home, healthy and well. When I arrived home my wife came to welcome me, and she said, 'Gordon is sick.' I said, 'I knew it, it has come at last.' Then there came that agonized struggle, 'Lovest thou me more than the boy?' But I had won the victory. So with a heavy heart I went up to the lad to say good-bye.

He lay on his bed, his little white face against the pillow, desperately ill. There I realized that the only surrender which truly counts is the surrender unto death. I was able to say to God out of a full honesty of heart, 'Thy will is best, and I would rather have Thy will than anything on earth.' What happened then? It happened with me as with Abraham when he brought his son to the place of surrender unto death on Mount Moriah. God gave him back his boy—and mine."

Let us be willing to "Bind the sacrifice with cords to the horns of the altar."

SEVEN

The Cross and the Crucified One

Things did not go well in the home. The young man had an unhappy marriage. One day when they were out for a boat ride he accidentally (?) upset the boat and drowned his wife. But the law caught up with him and sentenced him to death for his crime. The last night before his execution his father was allowed to stay with him in his cell. The next morning the authorities led the son out to death.

A few moments later they called for the old, heartbroken father. As he stood there over the poor lifeless frame of his boy, he said, "Oh, my son, if only I could impart to you my life—if only I could put my life into you that you might become the man I had intended you to be." Even so, Christ has for me an abundant fullness of life. He yearns over me that I may become partaker of His own divine nature—

that I may become the Christian He has intended me to be.

To this end Jesus Christ took on Him not the nature of angels, but the seed of Abraham, coming in my very frame and form. In the likeness of my own humanity, my very own, He took me up with Himself into the place of execution. Yes, He died my death. In His death I was discharged from sin, or, as Paul says, "justified from sin." In Christ's dead body I behold sin's claim and power exhausted. With Christ I have been jointly crucified. And just as "death no longer has dominion over Him," so God's promise to me is, "sin shall not have dominion over you" (Romans 6:9, 14). "In Christ" crucified, I died. "In Christ" risen, I am resurrected. But He carries every mark of His death into His resurrection. Without His death He would not be the resurrected One. He now lives as the Crucified One to make good the power and efficacy of His almighty death. And I am a "partaker of Christ," grafted into Him as the branch into the vine. "He that is joined unto the Lord is one spirit."

Did the first Adam, by virtue of my union with him, transmit to me the death-dealing effects of his disobedience? Yes, as truly does Christ transmit to me, by virtue of my life-union with Him, the vital effects of His obedience unto death. Christ died, not only for sin, but unto sin. In death He stripped sin of its last vestige of power. In the light of the Cross, sin's dominion is "no more."

In living realization of my union with Him, I should say to temptation a no that carries with it the power of the inward presence of the risen Lord. Far more, then, than any brokenhearted father, does the

Lord Jesus yearn to impart to us His own crucified-and-resurrected life—a life obedient unto death under the severest temptations and testings.

For certain kinds of murder, Roman law used to inflict an abominable and living death upon the red-handed criminal. He was fast-bound face-to-face to his victim until the murderer died. Only death released him from the carcass. In a similar manner Christ fastened me to Himself by cords of a love stronger than death and carried me to the Cross where, with Him, I was "jointly crucified."

In *Bone of His Bone*, F. J. Huegel reports that Mrs. Penn-Lewis recalled a missionary who "had a dream that greatly impressed him. It was of the Cross of Christ. However, it was not the Savior's bleeding form which held his eye. It was an exceedingly ugly thing, an indescribably loathsome thing, the nature of which he could not make out. What was this thing which so horrified him? Later, as he heard the message of identification, and realized that with Christ he had been crucified, the Spirit revealed to him that this loathsome thing he had seen in his dream was none other than himself."

But we cannot experience this truth of our union with Christ in death and resurrection by a mere lip profession or determined assertion. This life cannot be copied or possessed by resolution to practice Christ's presence. No imitation will avail. There must be a living participation by the Spirit through a new death to self. I cannot draw upon the life of the Crucified without admitting a new vital fellowship with Him in His death. I have the *new* life as I refuse the *old*—at the Cross. As I yield all to the power of His death I shall be "in the likeness of his resurrection." It is easy to work and fret and struggle and imagine that we are on the cross with Christ. In the energy of self we try to picture the nails driven hard into our flesh, thereby hoping to make vital the effects of His death. Such is the folly and futility of the flesh. A Christless cross is of no avail either to Protestant or Catholic. Others, brushing aside the death of Christ, try to live as He lived, to follow His example, to walk and talk and "be like Jesus." But a crossless Christ brings no vital union with Him. In order to have life we must be joined to Christ. And we can be joined to Him only in and through His death.

A Christless cross no refuge were for me;
A crossless Christ my Saviour could not be:
But, O Christ Crucified,
I rest in Thee!

But in coming to rest in Christ crucified as our life, our joy, our all, the Christian often goes through the bitter agonies of struggle and discouragement and defeat before coming to a glad consent to co-crucifixion. It is hard to unlearn self. Until we are sick unto death of sin, we have hard work to reckon ourselves dead unto sin. We practice all manner of self-crucifixion, but to no avail. Self dies hard.

In final captivity and thralldom to the "carcass" of self we are brought to cry out, "O wretched man that I am! who shall deliver me from the body of this death?" In such an hour the Lord Jesus bends over us, saying, "My son, let Me put the Spirit of life of My own resurrected being into you that you may 'be free indeed'—'free from the law of sin and death'—free to fulfill all that I have purposed you shall become." Oh, the blessed assurance that "if the Spirit of Him who raised Jesus from the dead dwells in you, He who raised Christ from the dead will also give life to your mortal bodies through His Spirit who dwells in you" (Romans 8:11). It is not self-crucifixion but union with Christ in His death and resurrection that lays the basis for Christian victory. The Crucified One *lives* to make real His own mighty death.

The story is told of a wealthy Christian merchant who had an only Son whom he loved dearly and who grew into noble young manhood. The father was wrapped up in his son's future and success. One night a boy who had led a criminal life from childhood broke into the home and attempted to kill the son. For days it seemed that the son would not live. But when he became conscious and was able to hear of what had occurred, he was shown the picture of the boy who had attempted to take his life. His heart was touched by the youthfulness of the lad. A desire was awakened in the son to try to save this lad from a life of crime. The father finally consented to the suggestion that the young criminal be taken into the home, adopted as a son and brother, and in time share the inheritance. It was with great difficulty that the young criminal was persuaded of their sincerity. Finally convinced, he agreed to their proposal.

Old habits, however, had such a hold upon him that time after time he fell back into evil ways, until the father almost despaired of ever being able to help him. But father and son, in spite of discouragement, held on and lavished their blessings upon him. One day at the height of his despair, the father went into the criminal boy's room and there noticed a picture of his own son. He picked it up and scanned it. The picture bore the marks of much thumbing and handling, and on the back of it was written, "Oh, I do so want to be like you, because you have done so much for me; but it seems as if I never can be good." Hope sprang up in the father's breast. His efforts were finally rewarded when the one-time criminal became "good."

Have you longed and sighed to be Christlike? You have said to the Lord Jesus, "Oh, I do so want to be like You, because You have done so much for me; but it seems as though I never can be good." Beloved, begin at once to reckon upon your death-resurrection position in Christ. Count by naked faith upon *the fact* of your union with Christ. In blind abandonment, as far as feelings are concerned, move out by a definite act of faith, trusting Christ to make real your life-union with Him. Sink your life into His, and let Him be your life, your light, your victory, your all.

Remember, your living, crucified Head is in heaven. *Head and members are one.* That is a fact of life. You and I are "bone of His bone." Let the glory of this vital union grip you, and you can never be the same again.

The rules of mathematics fail us here. Ordinarily one and one make two. But with God, one and one make one. "The two shall become one flesh." And

Paul explains, "This is a great mystery, but I speak concerning Christ and the church" (Ephesians 5:31–32). And "as the body is one and has many members, but all the members of that one body, being many, are one body, so also is Christ" (1 Corinthians 12:12). "The whole Christ includes both Head and body" (Augustine). Martin Luther made this practical observation: "The moment I consider Christ and myself as two I am gone."

Let us then be so experimentally one with Christ that we shall be one in interest, one in service, one in outlook—altogether one with the Crucified, having "two hearts that beat as one."

Dr. A. T. Pierson says: "A devout woman whom I once visited, to condole with her on the recent departure of an aged and most saintly mother, said to me with a smile: 'For forty years, my dear mother's mind has been in heaven.' And I could not but recall those exquisite lines of Goldsmith:

> *Like some tall cliff that lifts its awful form,*
> *Swells from the vale but*
> *   midway leaves the storm,*
> *Though round its breast*
> *   the rolling clouds are spread,*
> *Eternal sunshine settles on its head.*

Let our earthly dwelling place be amidst briars and thorns, and our skies be overcast. Faith feeds on the fact that "eternal sunshine settles" on our Head. Our "life is hidden with Christ in God" (Colossians

3:3). He and I are one, and "as He is [in yonder glory] so are we in this world" (1 John 4:17).

A letter just at hand from one of our graduates so well illustrates the truth that we quote it in part:

> I praise God for making known unto me that the riches of Christ are mine by grace, accomplished through the death and resurrection of Christ. So long I struggled to get to a place where it wouldn't be this everlasting up and down existence. I earnestly desired a victorious Christian life but the more I worked for it, the more miserable I became. I tried to attain unto it by prayers, obedience, resolutions and vows, but all to no avail. I had been saved from the guilt of sin by faith in Christ. Why should I have been so stupid as to think that by works I could be saved from the power of sin? The fact that my deliverance could come only *through faith,* as I appropriated the death and resurrection of Christ, never dawned upon my soul. Not until January of this year did the truth of my identification with Christ's death dawn upon me. I believe I saw for the first time what Paul meant when he said, "God forbid that I should glory, save in the cross of our Lord Jesus Christ, by whom the world is crucified unto me, and I unto the world." I praise the Lord for the Cross; for when all hope failed of ever shaking off the fetters of sin, through the Cross I rose victor over the power of sin. When nothing else could avail, death set me free.

EIGHT

The Cross
and Self

The church world is full of Christian professors
and ministers, Sunday school teachers and
workers, evangelists and missionaries in whom the
gifts of the Spirit are very manifest, and who bring
blessing to multitudes. However, when known
"close up," they are found to be full of self.

They may have "forsaken all" for Christ and
imagine they would be ready, like the disciples of
old, to die for their Master; but deep down in their
hidden, private lives there lurks that dark, sinister
power of self.

Such persons may wonder, all the while, why
they do not have victory over their wounded pride,
their touchiness, their greediness, their lovelessness,
their failure to experience the promised "rivers of
living water." Ah, the secret is not far away. They se-
cretly and habitually practice "shrine worship"—at

the shrine of self. There they bow daily and do obei-
sance. They are fundamental. In the outward Cross
they glory, but inwardly they worship another god
—and stretch out their hands to serve a pitied, pet-
ted, and pampered self-life.

The outward Cross, the payment of sin's penalty,
the death of the Substitute—this "finished work of
Christ"—they know. But the amazing mystery and
undreamed-of-depths of that Cross, as it is to be applied to the inner life,—"the mystery of the *inward* as
well as the *outward* Cross"—they know not. But,
notes F. J. Huegel (in *Cross of Christ*), "until Christ
works out in you an inner crucifixion which will cut
you off from self-infatuation and unite you to God in
a deep union of love, a thousand Heavens could not
give you peace."

> *God harden me against myself,*
> *The coward with pathetic voice*
> *Who craves for ease, and rest, and joys:*
>
> *Myself, arch-traitor to myself;*
> *My hollowest friend, my deadliest foe,*
> *My clog whatever road I go.*
>
> *Yet One there is can curb myself,*
> *Can roll the strangling load from me,*
> *Break off the yoke and set me free.*
>   *—Christina Rossetti.*

From his original home and center in God, where God was his light and life, the very breath of his breath, the central Sun of his universe—from this secret place of the Most High, man broke off and plunged out into the far country of self, into the alienation and night of separation from God. God has been cast down. Self has usurped the throne, a usurper who never abdicates. Self is the new and false center upon which man has fixed. He loves himself as nothing else under the sun. Even his best deeds are but refined forms, the filthy rags, of his secret selfishness. He does always with his right hand so that the left hand of self-satisfaction may know it. "Self," says William Law, "is the root, the branches, the tree of all the evils of our fallen state."

When this nearly almighty self unseated and dethroned El Shaddai, what could God do? He was scarcely taken by surprise. Yet how should He undo this tragedy of all tragedies? How would He unhinge and tear man loose from his foul and false self-infatuation? God must never coerce or force man. His supreme glory is an unforced worship. How dare He defeat His own divine purpose, His essential glory!

Herein is displayed the genius of God. The Cross is indeed "the power of God and the wisdom of God." Calvary is God's ax laid at the root of the first family tree. Adam is cut off. A new Adam ascends the throne.

The Lord Jesus came as the new Head of a new race. He willingly came, came in the likeness of sinful flesh. With cords of selfless love He fastened us to Himself and took us with Himself down to the very depths of death, all in order to clear away sin's penalty and persuade us to choose God instead of self. He chose to die—to die for us, to die in our place, yea, to die our death—that He might save us from our sinful selves.

Come, O fellow believer, the Son of man is made sin—made a curse—lifted up like a serpent.

"But," someone asks, "why a serpent? Why not a lily or a rose? Why not something lovely inasmuch as it was to typify the King and His redemptive work?" But when God would seek to picture the accursed character of the sinful self-life, He made no mistake. Only the serpent could symbolize the truth. That throws an awful ray of light upon me. It shoots me through and through. I am perfectly photographed—not my *sins* only, but *myself*. What I *did* only sprang from what I am. The unvarnished truth is out. It is I, my very self. Why pull down the blinds?

Let me take a square look at the Cross and be willing to abide by the awful implications.

> I see the crowd in Pilate's hall,
> I mark their wrathful mien;
> Their shouts of "Crucify!" appall,
> With blasphemy between.

> And of that shouting multitude
> I feel that I am one;
> And in that din of voices rude
> I recognize my own.

'Twas I that shed the sacred blood,
I nailed Him to the tree,
I crucified the Christ of God,
I joined the mockery.

Around the cross the throng I see
Mocking the Sufferer's groan;
Yet still my voice it seems to be
As if I mocked alone.
—Horatius Bonar.

Does such an admission seem too dreadful? Do I halt from owning it? But dare I disown it? Until I own it, I can never disown it. From the throne of the Cross, high and lifted up, I am drawn first to *own* and then *disown* self. I cease to speak about some of self and some of Christ. I am cursed, not cut back, but cut down, cut off. The connection is severed with all the past, and from self itself. I am simply consigned to the curse in toto. In the person of Another I have come to a lawful execution, an ignominious termination, and eternal undoing.

This judicial sentence calls for my most cordial acquiescence. Let me consent to my execution and sign on the dotted line. I have not been left to crucify myself. Such a task is too tremendous, too divine. I have been already devoted to death, "crucified with Christ." That has been accomplished. But I must sign my own death sentence. I must consent to God's consignment. I must choose, in the power of His

59

death, to dethrone and deny self. The Cross is indeed God's master weapon. But Christ's death has severing power only as we are united with it by faith. I must endorse this divine dying as it applies to me.

Such a denial of self is no mere severing of this or that indulgence, but putting the ax of the Cross to the very root of the tree of self. God says, "Cut the tree down," not merely trim it back. All self-righteousness, self-esteem, self-vindication, self-glory, and fatal self-pity—these and ten thousand other manifestations are but the fleshly foliage, the myriad branchings of that deeply rooted tree of self. To trim it back only means that the very life of self is thrown back into other more rugged roots, to develop the Pharisee into a more vigorous tree. Outwardly he may appear beautiful and be highly esteemed among men. But behind the scenes those living nearest him could bear tearful witness to that bitter fruit that flourishes on the green bay tree of self.

But there is abundant hope. I am already grafted into the Crucified One, a partaker of the divine nature. The life imparted to me is a crucified life, a life of death to self in its myriad forms. Self can never overcome self. But thank God I am already Christ-possessed. And, as I yield all to the Crucified One, His mighty death will work out in me an inner crucifixion. The more fully the Crucified has me, the more fully I must die to self.

Once someone asked George Mueller the secret of his service, and Mueller replied: "There was a day when I died"; and, as he spoke, he bent lower, until he almost touched the floor. Continuing, he added,

"Died to George Mueller, his opinions, preferences, tastes, and will; died to the world, its approval or censure; died to the approval or blame even of my brethren or friends; and since then I have studied only to show myself approved unto God."

> Though I be nothing, I exult
> In Thy divine perfection,
> And taste the deep, mysterious joy
> Of absolute subjection.
> Though I be nothing, I rejoice
> To find my all in Thee:
> Not I, but Christ forevermore:
> Amen! so let it be!
> —Lucy A. Bennett.

NINE

The Cross: Contrary to Nature

Mr. Spurgeon tells of a simple countryman who took his gun to the gunsmith for repairs. After examining it, the latter said: "Your gun is in a very worn-out, ruinous, good-for-nothing condition. What sort of repairing do you want for it?"

"Well," said the countryman, "I don't see as I can do with anything short of a new stock, lock, and barrel. That ought to set it up again."

"Why," said the smith, "you had better have a new gun altogether."

"Ah, I never thought of that. It strikes me that's just what I do want, a new stock, lock, and barrel. Why that's about equal to a new gun altogether, and that's what I'll have."

That is just what God says concerning poor human nature: "A new man altogether, and that's what I'll have."

But that poor, stupid countryman was sensible when compared with our reasoning in the things of the Spirit. It scarcely dawns upon us, even as God's children, that God's plan is to "cross" out the old race entirely. He says: "Behold, I make all things new." And in the infinite power of God and wisdom of God, He chose the Cross as the most complete contradiction of Adam's race—"that no flesh should glory in His presence" (1 Corinthians 1:29). The Cross contradicts our wills: Christ said, "Not My will, but Yours, be done." The Cross contradicts our wisdom: The wise of this world crucified the Lord of glory. The Cross contradicts our desires: "Those who are Christ's have crucified the flesh with its passions and desires" (Galatians 5:24). The Cross contradicts our pride: We are to let the mind be in us which was in Christ Jesus who humbled Himself and became "obedient to the point of death, even the death of the cross" (Philippians 2:8). The Cross contradicts self: "One died for all, then all died; and He died for all, that those who live should live no longer for themselves" (2 Corinthians 5:14–15).

The Cross contradicts human nature at every point. For the inexorable and unalterable terms of discipleship are these: Except a man denies himself, forsakes all that he has, "yes, and his own life also, he cannot be My disciple," Christ says.

When Christ went to the Cross, therefore, the "ax was laid to the root of the tree." The old Adamic stock—yes, lock, stock, and barrel—was done away. The Cross reveals our utter bankruptcy, and it pronounces a death sentence on Adam's race. It is God's master stroke to undo and drain away our natural life, that the life supernatural may take its place. Christ came not to straighten us out, but to "cross" us out; not to trim us back, but to cut us off; not to get us doing, but to bring us to an undoing. The Cross contradicts all fleshly doing and reveals a divine dying.

Christ came not to put new wine into old skins. He came not to put new cloth to an old garment, but to put off in toto the old man with his "duds." Hence the real meaning of Christ's command, "let him deny himself and take up his cross," can be nothing short of an ignominious termination and undoing of the whole of our moral and spiritual heritage from Adam. Such is the all-essential of our salvation, inasmuch as "self is the root, the tree, and the branches of all the evils of our fallen state" (Law).

It should be observed that self-denial is no mere cutting off of an indulgence here and there, but, as Dr. A. T. Pierson said, "laying the axe at the root of the tree of self, of which all indulgences are only greater or smaller branches. Self-righteousness and self-trust, self-seeking and self-pleasing, self-will, self-defense, self-glory—these are a few of the myriad branches of that deeply rooted tree. And what if one or more of these be cut off, if such lopping off of some few branches only throws back into others the self-life to develop more vigorously in them?" Until the ax, then, is laid to the root of the tree of self, and our natural life gives place to the life of the Spirit, all our "virtues are only taught practices grafted upon a corrupt bottom."

Is there not a tendency, however, even after we have been rooted in Christ, to be prompted more often than not from the old springs and roots of the tree of self? It is in this connection the Christian must learn the dynamic of the Cross as it applies to the believer. But let us illustrate. Jesus said: "I am the vine, you are the branches." As a branch of the old Adamic stock, I "brought forth wild grapes." As a partaker of Christ, I have been grafted into Him. When I believe *into* Christ crucified, I was cut off, cut away from my former natural connections, and grafted into Christ, the living Vine.

E. J. Pace says, "Some time ago near my home in Florida I visited a citrus nursery, and I asked the man in charge to show me how he grafted fruit. He led me to the grove of young trees. He then carefully cut from a little sapling a very small twig with a swelling bud at the end of it, and proceeding to another tree nearby he deliberately cut in the back of it a cross, and where the tree was expressly cut to receive it he deftly inserted the scion." Even so, we have been severed from our former family tree, and, at the Cross, grafted into the trunk of the eternal deity. Let faith fasten stoutly to this fact: I am a "joint heir" with Christ. We have become partakers of the divine nature.

However, ours is a grafting "contrary to nature." According to the ordinary laws of grafting, the good branch of a desirable fruit is grafted into an inferior trunk. Contrary to nature, we have been grafted into a good tree. The True Vine was crucified, and into the torn side of the Redeemer we have been grafted, a bad into a good.

There is another "contrary to nature" that is all-important. When the life-union of the vine and branch is effected in nature, the branch still bears

fruit "after its kind," i.e., according to its own original life. But I died in Adam. By the life I received
from Adam, I brought forth "fruit to death" (Romans
7:5). "The mind of the flesh is death." In order,
therefore, to bring forth fruit to God, this natural life
must give way, must "yield up the ghost." Having
been condemned to the Cross, I must come to feel
by a deep work of the Spirit that by nature I am unfit
to live. The Cross says so; and I must consent. I must
come to a cordial consent that I have been crucified
together with Christ, so that it is no longer I who
live, but Christ who lives in me. His crucified life
must come coursing through me, the ingrafted branch,
so contradicting and setting "me" aside, that the spiritual fruits of righteousness which are by Jesus Christ
—"after *His* kind"—shall be manifest to the glory
and praise of God.

Amy Carmichael tells about the nurse Kohila,
who, at a certain time, "came upon something in
herself which we call briefly *Nān thān. Nān* means I;
thān underlines the pronoun. Someone has said that
there is nothing God will not do through one who
does not care to whom the credit goes. *Nān thān*
greatly cares. Kohila set herself to renounce her *Nān
thān*, so that she might be free to serve others."
When Christ comes into the life He must "take over"
entirely; and He is on a sit-down strike until He starves
the "me" out.

The Cross must bring me to a glad "yet not I."
Contrary, then, to all the laws of grafting and fruit-
bearing, the "you-in-Me" of our life-union with
Christ is to be followed all our days by the "I-in-you"
of fruit-bearing.

Let us listen to the little scion as he repeats Galatians 2:20: "I have been cut off from my family tree; I am crucified to my former connection and family; I have been ruthlessly torn away; I am dead to them; nevertheless I live—I still know that I am the same little wild branch and no other—*I am still myself.* I live. And yet it is no longer I that is living; it is the life of another that lives in me so that none of the beautiful grapes are of me. They are the product of the life of another, continually contradicting my old life and pushing on out through me to bear precious fruit to glorify the great husbandman."

In speaking of the violation of these principles of our fallen selfish natures, F. J. Huegel says: "We are so addicted to self, so wrapped up in self, so entwined with self, so infatuated with self, that our spiritual natures cannot be centered in God by means of a deep union of love without a violent contradiction of our old natures. This is the secret of the Cross. It does violence to corrupt human nature. It slays the old life."

Those who teach us that the blood of Jesus cleanses or eradicates the old nature often fail to enter into and learn the meaning of the Christ-indwelt life as the only lifelong remedy for self. It was the saintly Francis de Sales who said, "It is a delusion to seek a sort of ready-made perfection which can be assumed like a garment; it is a delusion, too, to aim at a holiness which costs no trouble, although such holiness would be no doubt exceedingly agreeable to nature. We think that if we could discover the secret of sanctity we should become saints quickly and easily." We shall the rest of our lives be making new and fresh discoveries of plague spots in our nature upon which the Cross must be laid. Has the reader not discovered, in spite of many victories over self and sin, how many natural choices and likes and preferences need to have the death-mark of Calvary put upon them? The birthmark of nature must be contradicted throughout by the death-mark of the Cross. Let us, then, ask the Lord to mark His Cross upon all our natural choices.

But, thanks be to God, this yet-not-I kind of a Christian life is no lifelong funeral procession. Nay, verily, for Jesus said, "He who loses his life for My sake *will find it*" (Matthew 10:39; italics added). What could be more wonderful than that the Son of God, glorious and eternal, Creator of all things, "who loved me and gave Himself for me," should stoop to make me His own, His very temple? Has He not promised, "Because I live, you will live also" (John 14:19)?

Oh, the marvel and mystery of "you in me" and "I in you"! The branch is in the Vine and the Vine is in the branch. Glorious life-union of life and love and liberty! I am made alive together with Him, raised together with Him, seated together with Him. I am rooted in the Eternal, with my life already "hidden with Christ in God." If the roots of our life are in our risen Lord, we shall "be neither barren nor unfruitful in the knowledge of our Lord Jesus Christ" (2 Peter 1:8).

Have we had the bitter experience of trying to produce fruit? We have toiled and tried and prayed and bled, but all to no avail. In spite of all our efforts, the stream of our life is mixed and muddy through our own unholy duplicity of motives. We know that in Christ there is abundant fullness. The question is how to get it out.

With Hudson Taylor we say, "I knew full well that there was in the root abundant fullness; but how to get it into my puny little branch was the question." In a veritable paroxysm of despair we finally cry out, "O wretched man that I am! Who will deliver me from this body of death?" Thank God there is a life all-divine and powerful that can contradict and liberate and set us free: "I thank God—through Jesus Christ our Lord! . . . For the law of the Spirit of life in Christ Jesus has made me free from the law of sin and death" (Romans 7:24–25; 8:2).

TEN

The Cross and the Two Natures

D. M. Panton once noted: "A wild man, if imprisoned in a cage, so long as he is alone, is gentle, tractable, quiet, and appears quite civilized and reasonable; alone in the cage, he follows his own will, and has his own way, and is at peace. But unlock the door and push a civilized man into the cage and watch. The wild man's countenance changes; an angry scowl darkens his face; and in another moment he hurls himself on the intruder, and the two are locked in deadly conflict."

A close fellow worker once said: "I didn't know I had a temper until after I was saved." Until then her house had not been divided against itself. Self was in complete control. She chose her own path; she went her own way; she followed her own will. When, however, she became "a new creature" in Christ, she began to discover the poisonous principle of selfishness which was lodged in us at the Fall.

The Savior said plainly to religious Nicodemus: "That which is born of the flesh is flesh"—it can never enter the realm of spirit. It is unconvertible, incurable, incorrigible. Only "that which is born of the Spirit is spirit" (John 3:6). There is, therefore, in each believer the old man and the new. When Scripture speaks of the "first man," the "natural man," and "the old man which is corrupt according to the deceitful lusts," it refers to what we are "in Adam," and from him by nature. On the other hand, those who have been born again have become new creatures "in Christ"; they have put on "the new man."

As a believer I am shocked when I first discover "that in me (that is, in my flesh) nothing good dwells" (Romans 7:18). The mind of the flesh is death. "It is not subject to the law of God, nor indeed can be" (Romans 8:7). It is unmitigated antagonism against the things of the Spirit. It is not merely an enemy, in which case it might be reconciled. But it is *enmity* against God." Paul says: "The flesh lusts against the Spirit, and the Spirit against the flesh; and these are contrary to one another" (Galatians 5:17).

But the most startling and distressing shock to me personally is to find that *I am both*: "I am carnal, sold under sin," and "I delight in the law of God according to the inward man" (Romans 7:14, 22). Most every sincere Christian will therefore at some time or another cry out, consciously or unconsciously, "O wretched man that I am! Who will deliver me from this body of death?"

This war, according to Scripture and experience, is of all wars the very worst. It is a civil war—a war not with an external foe but with an internal "fifth column" invading the very citadel of one's soul. It is wrong to suppose that this relentless and undying antagonism can settle down to a deadlock, a kind of stalemate where neither side wins. We also fear that many Christians, having adopted what might be termed a *defeatist* position, attempt to make "the old man" responsible for their daily misdeeds.

Christians have doubtless been encouraged in this extreme on account of certain teachers who give the impression that "the regenerate man is made up of two persons, two individuals, the old man and the new man, constituting two separate and independent beings, an angel and a devil linked together— the old man unchangeably evil, the new perfect and impeccable" (H. Bonar). On the contrary, I am a single individual. As such I am responsible to "put off the old" and to "put on the new." The old man and the new man are not separate and distinct persons, but simply two aspects of one single responsible individual. Bishop Moule says: "And the body is no separate and, as it were, minor personality. If the man's body 'machinates' it is the man who is the sinner."

In an earlier chapter we noted that Emperor William once refused a request for an audience prepared by a German-American. The ground on which the audience was refused was this: Germans born in Germany but naturalized in America became Americans: "I know Americans, I know Germans, but German-Americans I do not know." As an individual I was once "in Adam." That same individual is now "in Christ." Make no mistake about it, I cannot at the same time be "in Adam" and "in Christ."

When I was in Adam, I was "in the flesh," lost and cursed and in no sense a Christian. But I was cut off from Adam and joined to Christ in vital life—union *at the Cross*. Through my union with Christ, I am "not in the flesh, but in the Spirit." We emphasize it again, therefore, that those who have been *born* again are not Adam-Christ believers. Such an approach will permit me no audience with my King. The Old Testament criminal who, in order to escape the law, "fled unto the tabernacle of the Lord, and caught hold on the horns of the altar," had meted out to him his just deserts: "You shall take him from My altar, that he may die" (1 Kings 2:28 KJV; Exodus 21:14). Even so, all flesh is under the curse. Our old man was crucified with Him. We fear that many believers are holding the truth of the two natures in such a way that forbids audience with the King. On what grounds do we seek access to the throne? There is no mercy for the flesh. It dare not approach the holy place, lest God say, "Take him from My altar that he may die." We must go in as crucified or not go at all. The Cross has fixed an eternal separation between us and the old man. Be this my lifelong attitude! Only thus can I go in "by the blood of Jesus."

It has often been true of a Jewish or Hindu convert to Christianity that the relatives, in order to express how completely they cast him out, actually celebrate his funeral. Henceforth they treat him as though he no longer exists. We once heard a Jewish Christian thus describe his own "burial." Just after that funeral had been celebrated, the father made as though he would kiss the son good-bye. But the mother stepped between the two and said to the father, "Would you kiss that dead dog?" When Christ came into my humanity, He fastened me to Himself and took me to the cursed tree and down into the tomb that He might "once-for-all" terminate my relationship to my "old man." Having been buried, I am "married to another, even to him who is raised from the dead." Has it ever dawned upon me what an ethical and moral contradiction I am to the Bridegroom of my soul when I step back to "kiss that dead dog"? Let me, then, solemnly sign my death sentence, and forever celebrate the funeral!

Not long ago we were preaching along this line when a perfect "dandy" commented after the message, "I don't know what he was talking about; I am not as bad as all that." A friend said: "Do you mean that you are never bothered with envy or vanity or pride?" (Such things were all too manifest.) "Oh yes, of course," he replied. "Well, what do you do about those things?" Glibly he replied, "Oh, the Blood takes care of all that."

To this poor, self-sufficient young Christian, sin has not yet "become exceeding sinful." In the meantime the Lord Jesus is indeed a convenient fire escape out of hell, and His blood a handy rinse, absolving this superficial Christian of all responsibility.

Note again the close connection between the *justification* of Romans 5 and the *sanctification* of Romans 6, the one laying the basis for and leading immediately into the other. Concerning the former Paul says, "Where sin abounded, grace abounded much more." Concerning the latter he asks, "What shall we say then? Shall we continue in sin that grace may abound? Certainly not! How shall we who died to sin live any longer in it?" (Romans 5:20; 6:1, 2). The apostle then proceeds to explain that, when we were justified in Christ, we were so united with Him, "baptized into His death," that our whole former connection with Adam and with sin was forever terminated.

In His death, Christ placed between my old man and the new "the immeasurable depths of Calvary's annihilations. In view of my life-union with Christ crucified, I am vitally involved in that death. It is *my* judicial standing. From it issues the life I live—a life of death *unto* sin and *oneness* with God" (Huegel). This is my position the moment I become a Christian.

While there is no scriptural reason why the justified believer should not, immediately upon conversion, reckon himself "dead indeed to sin, but alive to God through Jesus Christ our Lord," the fact remains that most of us wander, as did the apostle Paul, in the wilderness of a divided affection (Romans 7) until we learn that "in me (that is, in my flesh) nothing good dwells." But once we cry out in utter hopelessness and despair, "O wretched man that I am! Who will deliver me from this body of death," then we enter into the blessed land of fruitful obedience—and conflict.

Ah yes, the conflict remains in Romans 8, but oh, how different! In Romans 7 Paul experienced a conflict which issued in the most tragic defeat. That chapter is full of "I" and "me." In Romans 8 the conflict continues, but with Paul on the winning side. "The Spirit of life in Christ Jesus" has made him free.

But note that Paul stands in Romans 8 at the fork of two roads. To the left is the path "after the flesh"; to the right "after the Spirit." These two paths continually face the most victorious Christian. It is ours to choose. In Romans 8 the believer has liberty to choose to walk "after the Spirit." But it is not liberty that is automatic. We must still choose.

Thank God "we are debtors—not to the flesh, to live according to the flesh" (v. 12). That is glorious encouragement. The old debtorship has been canceled. Then Paul couples warning with encouragement in verse 13: "For if you live according to the flesh you will die." The phrase "you will die" has been variously rendered, "about to die," "on the way to die," and "doomed to die." Is this what James means when he warns those drawn away by their own lust that "sin, when it is full-grown, brings forth death"?

Most good expositors see here a frightful warning to those who continue to walk "after the flesh." Reliable Matthew Henry says: "In a word, we are put upon this dilemma, either to displease the body or destroy the soul." Jamieson, Faucett, and Brown say in that most excellent commentary, "If *ye* do not kill sin, it will kill you." Instead, therefore, of likening this undying conflict to a kind of deadlock or stalemate, the apostle rather likens it to a duel where *each is out to take the life of the other.*

After the children of Israel had gone through Jordan's floods (a figure of our death and resurrection with Christ) and had entered into the land of *fruit* and *fight,* they were indeed put upon the dilemma: "If you do not kill the Canaanites, they will kill you."

In this analogy is set forth the warfare between the flesh and the Spirit. While not ignoring the dark side of these warnings, we would rather thank God for the bright alternative that concludes verse 13: "If by the Spirit you put to death the deeds of the body, you will live."

ELEVEN

The Cross
and Dying to
the Old Nature

In this chapter we wish to give special, though brief, consideration to that much discussed and difficult portion, 1 John 3:6–9:

> Whoever abides in Him does not sin. Whoever sins has neither seen Him nor known Him. Little children, let no one deceive you. He who practices righteousness is righteous, just as He is righteous. He who sins is of the devil, for the devil has sinned from the beginning. For this purpose the Son of God was manifested, that He might destroy the works of the devil. Whoever has been born of God does not sin, for His seed remains in him; and he cannot sin, because he has been born of God.

We have never been satisfied with what we feel to be forced explanations of this passage. Most all seem so colored by doctrinal preconceptions as to miss the purpose of the epistle. John wrote this epistle in order to bring God's children into an experimental "fellowship . . . with the Father and with His Son Jesus Christ" (1 John 1:3). The conditions of such a fellowship are practical as well as severe, and they center around proper believing and behaving.

John says: "My little children, these things I write to you, so that you may not sin. And if anyone sins, we have an Advocate with the Father, Jesus Christ the righteous" (1 John 2:1). The "holiness" man, so called, places most all his emphasis upon the first part of the verse; the rest of us on the latter.

Let us first clean up our own house before we throw stones. We repeat the wise words of Dr. A. J. Gordon: "Divine truth as revealed in Scripture seems often to lie between two extremes. . . . Almost all of the gravest errors have arisen from adopting some extreme statement of Scripture to the rejection of the other extreme. . . . If we regard the doctrine of sinless perfection as a heresy, we regard contentment with sinful imperfection as a greater heresy."

John wrote, "Let no one deceive you. He who practices righteousness is righteous" (3:7). John seeks to correct those believers who boast of righteousness "in Christ" while still "continuing in sin." "In Christ" and "in sin" do not go together. John says, "In Him there is no sin," (v. 5) and therefore to be abiding in Him is not to be sinning. He then climaxes this argument with the verse that "Whoever has been born of God does not sin, for His seed remains in him; and he cannot sin, because he has been born of God."

Would John be satisfied with our usual explanation that the general bent of the Christian life is rather characteristically good? That is a general truth. Yet a man may be a generally good Christian while still having no vital fellowship with God, such as John has in mind. Such an explanation makes no point in keeping with the purpose of the epistle, which is to bring the already regenerated into abiding fellowship with God. Again, was John thinking of the suggestion that the believer sins not with his new man, but only with the old? We believe not. Finally, did John have in mind those who have been so eradicated that they automatically do not sin? Surely not.

First of all notice that the phrase, "has been born of God," is in the present perfect tense. John refers not to the believer's past regeneration. John does not say the believer "cannot sin, because he was born of God." John is dealing with the present tense and the condition upon which the already regenerated may experience fellowship. But to be more practical, John says to me as I face a moral choice, that, if I "am born" with the living seed of God's Word, then I "cannot sin" in that given respect. The phrase "cannot sin" had perfect illustration when Joseph faced the choice (Genesis 39) of walking after the flesh or after the Spirit. He cried: "How then can I do this great wickedness, and sin against God?" (v. 9). God's word of promise Joseph so hid in his heart—"his seed [remained in] him" (Genesis 17:19)—that he "fled and ran outside"(v. 12). In that given instance Joseph certainly "sinned not." Joseph said in substance, "I have been born of God; I cannot sin."

Throughout life we shall be coming to similar forks of the road where we must daily choose between the flesh and the Spirit, between the old and the new. At that fork, we face our cross—daily. New duty will demand, as it were, a new death and resurrection. This will be the way the believer "is begotten" to "walk in newness of life." New light will continually break on the pathway, demanding a new step of obedience.

Now shall we return, as it were, to the land of Canaan, the land of fruit and fight? When the Israelites entered that land, that blessed land of obedience, was it not already theirs by inheritance? In the same way believers have been given "all spiritual blessings" in Christ. But to us, as to Joshua, comes the promise, "Every place that the sole of your foot will tread upon I have given you." Joshua must plant his foot upon the necks of his enemies. And believers today must "put to death the deeds of the body."

But did God hold Israel responsible for taking the whole of that land at once? Decidedly, no. In fact, He said: "I will not drive them out before you in one year. . . . Little by little I will drive them out from before you, until you have increased, and you inherit the land" (Exodus 23:29–30). Even so with us. We are to be all our days taking new territory, first in our own lives and then in "the regions beyond." Again, Israel faced "seven nations greater and mightier" than herself. How could she ever overcome but by the Almighty? Even so with us. The old life is too strong for us. But the promise is, "If by the Spirit you are doing to death (observe the present tense; the process is a continuing one), the practices, the stratagems, the machinations of the body, you will live" (Moule). God says to Israel and to us that in this way we shall possess our possessions.

But let us proceed. The first impossible fortress to face Israel was Jericho. But "by faith the walls of Jericho fell down," and Joshua "utterly destroyed all that was in the city" (Hebrews 11:30; Joshua 6:21). Now the question is appropriate, Was Israel to fight and take Jericho every other day?

Nay, verily. "Having overcome all," they were "to stand." They were simply to "abide" in the victory already won. In that particular and to that degree they sinned not.

In a similar manner we should take definite fortresses—such as laziness, covetousness, selfishness and self-ease and self-indulgence (perhaps long entrenched)—and having planted the Cross there on that bit of the old life, "stand." That is taken, therein abide. It is only compromise and false leagues of peace with the cursed Canaanites that make it necessary to fight and retake (and perhaps never take?) certain "high places" where Satan holds sway with his "chariots of iron."

Mount Jebus once defied and mocked David and his men. That fortress had stood out for some four hundred years against Israel, "Nevertheless David took the stronghold of Zion." It became his capital city. From that point, he reigned over all. Is there some one point in the reader's life that defies entrance? By the greater Son of David, scale that height, cast out the foe, and see how you will "reign in life by one, Jesus Christ." John says the same, "For whatever is

born of God overcomes the world" (1 John 5:4).
What is the next place in your world to overcome?

Daily the believer faces the Cross. Through that
death-resurrection process, he "is born" into newness
of life, both for fruit and for fight. As he walks in the
light, overcomes at each new crisis of obedience,
and there learns "to stand," to that degree (all that
God requires for fellowship at the moment), he is assured by Paul as well as John, "Walk in the Spirit,
and you shall not [in any way] fulfill the lust of the
flesh" (Galatians 5:16).

Beloved, can we imagine disobedient Israel
boasting, while bleaching her bones in the wilderness, that she had everything up in Canaan? What
glory then is it for the double-minded believer, wan-
dering in the wilderness of a divided affection, to
boast continually that he has everything "in the
heavenly places in Christ"—all the while taking no
territory for Christ, experiencing no milk and honey
and grapes, and grappling with no foes for his Redeemer? Any "stalemate" conception of the two natures will not stand the test of Scripture. You are no
Adam-Christ believer. Do you believe in suppression? God did not say to put Canaanites to tribute,
to keep them tied up. They were to be put, not to
tribute, but to death. Are you an eradicationist with
all fruit and no fight? Your position is contrary to
Scripture and to your own experience. Both posi-
tions are untenable.

The Cross has the solution. We have been crucified with Christ—have "put off" the old man. Now
put him out, i.e., "mortify" his deeds. Apply His
death. Let the Cross shame and crucify you out of

any position of unholy duplicity. "Purify your hearts, you double-minded" (James 4:8). The Cross condemns us to live like saints. Hallelujah! Let us go up at once and possess. We be well able "through the Spirit."

A word of encouragement for those who have slipped—and who has not? The only remedy is to confess your sins at once. The propitiation is ours. Remember also that the blood avails for the sins of ignorance and the many failures. But let our attitude be forever that of John: "that we sin not."

O fellow believer: "There remains very much land yet to be possessed" (Joshua 13:1). Let us lift up our eyes and behold the fields white unto harvest. We have dwelt at length upon the great stretches of territory untaken in our own lives. But we would fall woefully short of God's program and purpose in this chapter if we did not give our thought to the vast unoccupied fields in all the world. Oh, to get over the "civil war" that we may go into all the world and win for the Lamb the reward of His sufferings! The great Shepherd of the "other sheep" who commanded us, "Occupy till I come" must be in agony over those other sheep concerning whom He Himself said, "Them also I must bring."

There is perhaps no single point upon which the church of Jesus Christ is so utterly disobedient to the command of her crucified Lord as upon the subject of "missions." The Canaanites of covetousness and laziness—the sins of omission are greater often than the sins of commission—have killed the forward march of the church. The church as a whole is "living after the flesh"—and dying, going into atrophy and death. From Dr. Glover's *Progress of Worldwide Missions* we would quote the following by a well-known missionary leader, the Rev. Charles R. Watson, President of the American University at Cairo:

> The occupation of all the unoccupied fields is the distinctive and crowning challenge of this missionary age. Upon the church's acceptance of that challenge great issues seem to depend: issues affecting the vitality of the Christian Church, issues determining the welfare and happiness of millions of our fellow creatures, issues conditioning the lives of nations, issues upon which God Himself has been pleased to hang the unfolding of His eternal purposes in Christ. The unoccupied fields must be occupied, and what is the price of their occupation? The pathway which leads to their occupation lies across other unoccupied fields—great areas these—in our own lives and hearts, not yet surrendered to the will of Christ, not yet fully occupied by His Spirit, not yet touched by the flame of a perfect love and consecration. Only as He is permitted to fully occupy these nearer areas in our own lives will He be able to gain entrance into those more distant fields of the unoccupied world.

TWELVE

The Cross
and
the Flesh

If the flesh could speak as it faces the Cross, it would be forced to use the language of one man Amiel (as quoted by Amy Carmichael). After he had received at the hands of his doctors the verdict which was to him the sentence of death, he said,

> On waking, it seemed to me that I was staring into the future with wide-startled eyes. Is it indeed to *me* that these things apply? Incessant and growing humiliation, my slavery becoming heavier, my circle of action steadily narrower? What is hateful is that deliverance can never be hoped for, and that one misery will succeed another in such a way as to leave me no breathing space, not even in the future, not even in hope. All possibilities are closed to me, one by one.

To the flesh, the Cross is God's verdict, God's "sentence of death." Paul traveled a long road to learn "that in me (that is, in my flesh,) nothing good dwells."

"Is it indeed to *me*," cries the awakened believer, "that these very things apply?" It does seem to take a long time to learn that the mind of the flesh "is enmity against God." It is therefore "not subject to the law of God, nor indeed can be" (Romans 8:7). The verdict has gone forth, the sentence executed. The only cure is condemnation, crucifixion, death with Christ. The flesh with all its foul brood has been put to the hanged man's doom. To the accursed tree, Christ nailed "the flesh with its passions and desires." There Christ reversed all the processes of nature; the old life was terminated to make room for the new, for death can never inherit life. And "the mind of the flesh is death." The flesh has about it "the smell of infernal associations. It stinks." Since its mind is already death, God sent it to its own place—the Cross.

In speaking of "the flesh" as contrary to "the Spirit," Scripture refers to the whole of human nature in its fallen condition. We read of the *wills* of the flesh, the *desires* of the flesh, the *mind* of the flesh, the *wisdom* of the flesh, the *purposes* of the flesh, the *confidence* of the flesh, the *filthiness* of the flesh, the *workings* of the flesh, the *warring* of the flesh, and the *glorying* of the flesh. Scripture mentions those who walk according to the flesh, after the flesh, make a fair show in the flesh. Man's emotions, his reasonings, his powers—all his thinking and willing and energy—are under the lordship of the flesh.

The flesh must go to the Cross. It must be made to face the fact and made to say that "deliverance can never be hoped for, all possibilities are closed to me in such a way as to leave me no breathing space, not even in the future, not even in hope. It is to me these very things apply." The Cross seizes hold of man's fleshly self-life, and carries it to judgment, a judgment so final that it spells death.

Amiel indeed felt it "difficult for the natural man to escape from a dumb rage against" such an inexorable arrest. It is worse than difficult; it is impossible. But with God, the impossible becomes possible. Those who have been born again have gone through this judgment in the person of Christ. To the unbeliever, God says; "They that are in the flesh cannot please God." But to us He says, "You are not in the flesh, but in the Spirit." We are assured as His that "those who are Christ's have crucified the flesh with its passions and desires." And as we yield ourselves continually unto God, as those who are alive from the dead, we experience that liberty with which Christ has made us free. The word of assurance is that, "if the Spirit of Him who raised Jesus from the dead dwells in you, He who raised Christ from the dead will also give life to your mortal bodies through His Spirit who dwells in you. Therefore, brethren, we are debtors [and he seems about to say to the Holy Spirit; but he turns to say]—not to the flesh, to live according to the flesh" (Romans 8:11–12).

The flesh has been judged and our position is "in the Spirit."

Even though the believer has emerged from the muddle and mixedness of Romans 7 through Paul's command to "reckon yourselves also to be dead indeed to sin," the fact remains that he will discover many ways in which self seeks satisfaction through the as-yet-unredeemed spheres of his being. The flesh, the body, all "our mortal coil" is evidently still present in Romans 8. That chapter presents many ways in which death to our flesh must set in. The victorious believer will become aware of many forms of self which must yet be dealt with. We shall discover:

- in our service for Christ, self-confidence and self-esteem;
- in the slightest suffering, self-saving and self-pity;
- in the least misunderstanding, self-defense and self-vindication;
- in our station in life, self-seeking and self-centeredness;
- in the daily routine, self-pleasing and self-choosing;
- in our relationships, self-assertiveness and self-respect;
- in our education, self-boasting and self-expression;
- in our desires, self-indulgence and self-satisfaction;
- in our successes, self-admiration and self-congratulation;
- in our failures, self-excusing and self-justification;
- in our spiritual attainments, self-righteousness and self-complacency;

- in our public ministry, self-reflection and self-glory.

Finally, in our life as a whole, we will discover self-love and selfishness. The flesh is an "I" specialist.

These are but a few of the multiple forms of "the flesh" to be discovered and taken to the Cross.

Mantle explained how one foreign palace reflected the self:

> In the Palace of Wurtzung there hangs a hall of glass. It is called the Hall of a Thousand Mirrors. You enter —a thousand hands are stretched out to meet you, a thousand smiles greet your smile, a thousand eyes will weep when you weep; but they are all your hands, your smiles, your tears. What a picture of the selfish man! Self all round, self multiplied, and he is deceived.

It is of God's wisdom that we should not be burdened with the discovery of these many forms of the flesh life all at once. Although emancipated at the life-center of our redeemed beings through the indwelling and infilling of the Spirit of life in Christ Jesus, we are still in a fight—albeit on the victory side. Vast areas of the flesh must yet be crucified. We must become Christlike. As an old black Christian in Africa put it: "The Cross of Christ condemns me to become a saint."

Calvary's floods of death are between us and that world. We have been crucified with Christ. There let us stand. Be consistent. Why halt between two opinions? Why be double-minded? Why make provision for the flesh? Why not pay your last respects to the flesh? We are debtors, thank God, not to the flesh to live after the flesh.

You are His? Then be His. Be what you are. Be out and out. Obey God. When God says, "Pluck out," don't try to salve your conscience with prayer. When God says, "Cut off," crying will not do.

We are largely creatures of habit. By birth we are selfish, and by long practice we have lived to please ourselves. We have long been debtors to certain fleshly tendencies. We have settled down perchance (wicked notion) that it must be ever thus. There are certain Canaanites who "would dwell in the land." They have chariots of iron. Let us set out a few of the more common and subtle forms of the flesh which are manifest "hangovers" in many Christians.

You may always have been a murmuring, complaining Christian. You sulk and feel sorry for your "sad, sweet self." But you need not do so. "If the Spirit of Him who raised Jesus from the dead dwells in you," He will so quicken your poor mortal, murmuring frame that you will experience the power of the Cross to cancel the complaining. There is a point to be observed, however; the victory will not be automatic. It will be only: "If by the Spirit [note that you must co-operate] you put to death the deeds of the body" (Romans 8 :13).

You are sensitive, "thin-skinned"? Why not call it sinful pride? The next time somebody reproves you, just say, "You don't know half the truth. If you knew me, you would say much worse." This may help you into harmony with the Cross. It will at least be the truth.

The flesh reasons that if your circumstances were only different you could have victory. But circumstances only reveal what is inside. Our insistence here is this: that "the eternal substance of a thing never lies in the thing itself, but in the quality of our reaction toward it. If in hard times we are kept from resentment, held in silence, and filled with inward sweetness, that is what matters. The event that distressed us will pass from memory as a wind that passes and is gone. But what we were while the wind was blowing upon us has eternal consequences" (Amy Carmichael).

You may be a zealous Christian. But have you gotten over a fleshly itch for a thrilling baptism of power? Do you demand signs and wonders before you will believe? The flesh seeks to glory in God's very presence. Those who make such imperious demands upon God keep alive the very fleshly, selfish principle which must go to the Cross. In Old Testament ceremony, the blood, representing death, always preceded the anointing with oil, representing the Spirit. Do we forget that the Spirit comes from the Crucified in heaven? Five bleeding wounds He bears. They still proclaim that the flesh with its passions and desires was crucified. Nadab and Abihu once offered strange fire before God—and died.

Are you given to gossip? The principle of curiosity is like the troubled sea that cannot rest. Does your tongue cast up a world of mire and dirt? We know a true minister who sought to control his tongue by taking a red hot poker and searing it. But the trouble was deeper. It was a heart matter. However, his attitude was right. He was willing to burn his tongue if that would help. He later learned how "through the Spirit" to put to death the deeds of the tongue.

Word just comes of a native preacher, until recently a flaming evangelist. His wife was self-assertive. In a certain issue she was manifestly wrong. But the preacher took sides with his wife. He has compromised with the flesh. Now, peace in the home is a wonderful thing, but not at such a price. The Spirit has ceased to use this preacher. Moreover, God gives drastic directions concerning such things when He says,

> "If your brother, the son of your mother, your son or your daughter, the wife of your bosom, or your friend who is as your own soul, secretly entices you, saying, 'Let us go and serve other gods . . . you shall not consent to him or listen to him, nor shall your eye pity him, nor shall you spare him or conceal him; but you shall surely kill him; your hand shall be first against him to put him to death, and afterward the hand of all the people. And you shall stone him with stones until he dies, because he sought to entice you away from the LORD your God." (Deuteronomy 13:6, 8–10)

This generation has been "graced" to spiritual softness and death. We do not "fear" as our forefathers did. We need the stiffening of Moses.

Has the reader noticed that when we ourselves are wrong we become very tender toward others who are wrong? The reason is that we want tender handling. "But syrupy affection," warned Amy Carmichael, "never yet led to spiritual integrity. And though it looks so like the charity which is greater than faith and hope, that it is 'admired of many,' it is not admirable. It is sin." Was the native preacher taken off his feet so easily because he was already unwatchful against the flesh? Did his wife only furnish the self-consideration for which he was already looking? The flesh gave "place to the devil." Satan is not divided against himself. Flesh always cliques up with flesh.

One of the most manifest forms of flesh is family flesh. Passing by the flesh that bites and devours one another, let us notice its subtler form. It is here that "syrupy affection" betrays the best of parents. Their fleshly attachment refuses to lead their children by the way of the Cross. Is it because the parents have not gone that way themselves?

A friend of the author passed away a few years ago. This lady had been brought up to believe that what she liked, her system needed and must have—whether it be food or clothing. She was not extravagant. Her life just centered in her likes and tastes and preferences. To these she daily bowed. She liked color, bright red especially. She liked fats and was very fond of sweets. She clung to these things as a cat clings to its home. They were her life. But the Savior said, "He who loves his life will lose it" (John 12:25). That is more than theology. It is a great fact, a principle of life; it is inexorable law. And it can be obtained even in this world.

The very things we lust after, hold to, and seek to save for ourselves, we lose. We lose those very things—find them distasteful to us, and that sooner than we think. Some months before passing away, color became unbearable to this lady. The flesh had to have bright red covered up. Her whole being revolted at fats. As to sweets—well, the least sugar became sickening. These had been her life. She had loved her life and refused to lose it—now she loathed it.

The Savior said: "Remember Lot's wife. Whoever seeks to save his life (*preserve it alive* is the thought) will lose it." Had Lot's wife not left Sodom? Indeed she had. But her flesh still fed on Sodom's sweets, and so she had not left it, had not lost it. To God, Sodom was only fit to be turned to a cinder; to Lot's wife it was still worth saving. She still sought to save her "life" from the falling fire—not her bodily life (for she was already outside the city)—but the things of her desire, the things of her world still back there in Sodom. She loved that life, longed for it, looked back and lost it—her life in Sodom, her bodily life, her all. There she stood, a pillar of salt, an eternal warning to those who live after the flesh.

My friend, the Lord is coming. What is your life? Is it lived in the Spirit? Oh, the power of the Cross to sever every relationship that would bind us to the flesh! We are debtors only to the Holy Spirit. Give the Cross full place in your life; abandon yourself recklessly to the Crucified One, for over His crucified life the flesh has not one speck of power. Let the Cross seize upon you and sever you from that dominating thralldom to the flesh. Every strong conviction ends by taking possession of us; it overcomes and absorbs us, and tears us ruthlessly from everything else.

Has the Cross so seized upon your life? If it has,

you can live for self nevermore. Rather, you will cry out with a determined saint of yore, "Oh my God, hear the cries of one on whom Thou hast had mercy, and prepare my heart to receive whatever Christ has purchased for me. Allow me not to rest short of it" (T. C. Upham).

We cannot better close this chapter than by quoting from that bed-ridden saint and soldier of India, Miss Amy Carmichael. She knew the pathway of suffering. She bore in her body the marks of the Lord Jesus:

> We who follow the Crucified are not here to make a pleasant thing of life; we are called to suffering for the sake of a suffering, sinful world. The Lord forgive us our shameful evasions and hesitations. His brow was crowned with thorns; do we seek rose-buds for our crowning? His hands were pierced with nails; are our hands ringed with jewels? His feet were bare and bound; do our feet walk delicately? What do we know of travail? of tears that scald before they fall? of heart-break? of being scorned? God forgive us our love of ease. God forgive us that so often we turn our faces from a life that is even remotely like His. Forgive us that we all but worship comfort, the delight of the presence of loved ones, possessions, treasure on earth. Far, far from our prayers too often is any thought of prayer for a love which will lead us to give one whom we love to follow our Lord to Gethsemane, to Calvary—perhaps because we have never been there ourselves.

THIRTEEN

The Cross
and
Relationships

Chrysostom says that when St. Lucian was asked by his persecutors, "Of what country art thou?" he replied, "I am a Christian."

"What is your occupation?"

"I am a Christian."

"Of what family?"

"I am a Christian."

To St. Lucian, Christ was all, whether of country, of occupation, or of family.

How revolutionary is the Cross! It revolutionizes all our relationships, toward God, toward ourselves, toward others, toward all. Once the Cross lays hold of the Christian, he realizes how completely un-hinged he has become from the whole of this present world. The old life, the old world, the old ways and relationships—all are past. "If any one is in Christ, he is a new creation; old things have passed away;

behold, all things have become new" (2 Corinthians 5:17). Such is the conviction of the Cross that it "takes possession of us; it overcomes and absorbs us, and tears us ruthlessly from everything else; it becomes our sole object, and outside it nothing seems to touch us; those who do not understand it are strangers to us; those who attack it are our enemies; those who love and serve it with us are our true, our only family."

"Do you suppose," warned the Savior, "that I came to give peace on earth? I tell you, not at all, but rather division. For from now on five in one house will be divided: three against two, and two against three. Father will be divided against son and son against father, mother against daughter and daughter against mother, mother-in-law against her daughter-in-law and daughter-in-law against her mother-in-law" (Luke 12:51–53). There is no divider like Christ. How He pierces and divides asunder! He "did not come to bring peace but a sword" (Matthew 10:34). His Cross sunders the dearest of earthly ties; violates our deepest attachments; gives us a heart of steel to ourselves and the tenderest of hearts toward others.

The Corinthians were Paul's children in the faith. In answer to their accusation that he did not love them, the great apostle and father said: "Open your hearts to us. We have wronged no one . . . for I have said before that you are in our hearts, to die together and to live together" (2 Corinthians 7:2–3). Note that Paul speaks "contrary to nature." Affectionate parents naturally want their children nearby to live and die with them. But Paul has already said to his Corinthian children: "Therefore, from now on, we regard no one according to the flesh" (5:16). The reason? "One died for all, then all died" (2 Corinthians 5:14). Paul therefore holds his children in his heart not to live and die with them, but to die and live with them. He knows them as Christ's. And if Christ's, they have been crucified and raised a new creation. Paul loves the Corinthians, but not "in the flesh." He loves them through the Cross. He knows "no man after the flesh."

Few Christian parents are governed by these simple implications of Calvary. We are thinking of our good Christian homes. Parents are often so wrapped up in their own children that they cannot bear to see them take the way of the Cross. They shield them from the path of suffering. Christian young people are often eager to go to all lengths for God and follow Christ to the ends of the earth, but the parents refuse to take the way of the Cross, either for themselves or for their children. "No one ever hated his own flesh," the apostle wrote the Ephesians (5:29). But it is the first law of discipleship, said Jesus, that "if anyone come to Me and does not hate his father and mother, wife and children, brothers and sisters, yes, and his own life also, he cannot be My disciple" (Luke 14:26).

Blood runs thick. Christian parents who have gone to great lengths in consecration and who seem otherwise to be sacrificial and devoted followers of Christ, break down at this point. Their fleshly sentiments make them, perhaps unconsciously, "the enemies of the cross of Christ." The Cross begins to lay hold of son or daughter and forthwith mother cries

out: "Far be it from you; this shall never happen!"
Happy the young person who so senses the serpent's
subtle and feigned love in that dreadful hour that he
can say: "Get behind Me, Satan! You are an offense
to Me, for you are not mindful of the things of God,
but the things of men" (Matthew 16:23).

We know a young woman called to China whose
mother warned her: "If you ever go to China, you
will go over my dead body." And she did. On her
deathbed the mother confessed: "Daughter is right; I
have been wrong." How sad to be forced to take the
divine order in death! The mother died; her daughter
went to China. The great Refiner and Purifier of sil-
ver sat over against the crucible of her deathbed and
skimmed off "the grey scum of selfishness" until
mother ceased to be a hindrance—albeit through the
doorway of death. She managed to rise to the miserable low of not refusing her daughter's call to China.

Concerning such parents, Amy Carmichael has
said: "Their high-water mark is expressed in such
words as these:

O Father, help, lest our poor love refuse
For our beloved the life that they would choose,
And in our fear of loss for them, or pain,
Forget eternal gain.

Another young lady was called of God to go to
India. Her mother was unsaved and seemed to need
her help. But the call of God had to come first; that
was unmistakable. Her Christian friends gave her

good advice according to the natural. They cautioned her that, if she were a real Christian, she would stay at home with her mother. But the daughter died—died to her own friends and her own good name. Counted as cruel and unloving, she was with her Master "reckoned among the transgressors." She trod the way of death. In harmony with the Crucified she went to India. Her mother was still over on the other side of the Cross, "dead in trespasses and sins." Calvary had come between daughter and mother.

But this is the divine order. Calvary not only divides; it draws. Christ was "set forth crucified" before the mother's eyes. Referring to Calvary, Jesus said: "I, if I am lifted up from the earth, will draw all peoples to Myself" (John 12:32). In a practical way Christ crucified was lifted up in that daughter—lifted up afresh to her mother. As Paul puts it: "before whose eyes Jesus Christ was clearly portrayed among you as crucified" (Galatians 3:1). Mother saw the Crucified One, for her daughter had been "crucified with Christ." The daughter had her mother in her heart, not to live and die with her, but "to die and live." God honors those who so die to honor Him. In time this daughter came home on her first furlough and led her mother to Christ. She saw her fall asleep in Jesus and quietly laid away—and went back in the will of God to India.

Another case. A prodigal son was determined to "have a fling." His mother was a woman of prayer. He comforted himself beneath her prayers that he could not get far away. At length the mother detected a fatal flaw in her own praying. Her sentiment would save her son from the way of transgressors, which is hard. She was not in full identification with the spirit of the Cross. At length she came to have her son in her heart "to die and live" with him. She warned him: "Son, I'm no longer asking God to protect you or save you from trouble; I am asking Him to get you, dead or alive."

Oswald Chambers says: "Whenever we step back from identification with God's interest in others into sympathy with them, the vital connection with God has gone; we have put our sympathy, our consideration for them in the way; and this is a deliberate rebuke to God." That son is a missionary in Africa today. He got afraid of mother's prayers. Shall I say that "mother *died*"—died to her own fleshly attachment? Her son then followed her through the Cross into resurrection life and service.

In the days of the Scottish Covenanters, in those times before an enervating effeminacy had overtaken our faith, Jane Welsh, the noble daughter of John Knox, was approached by the prison officials with the assurance that her husband, John Welsh, would be freed only if he would renounce the Protestant faith. Gathering up her apron she replied, "Please your majesties, I would rather catch his head there." Our modern sentiment would call her intolerant, dogmatic, unloving. But she truly loved God first, and her husband as herself. She had suffered much for the faith through her husband's imprisonment, but she still had him in her heart to die and live with him.

There is nothing so terrible, nothing so revolutionary as the Cross. But it is God's place of victory for ourselves and for our relatives—"as dying, and, behold, we live . . ."

FOURTEEN

The Cross, Suffering, and the Will of God

I am thinking of a poor little lassie of India, Mimosa by name. She heard one brief message concerning the love of the great Creator—how that love had been manifested in redemption. Prior to then, "she knew just nothing; there had not been time to tell her." She was hastened away by a cruel father, lest she become like her sister, Star, who was in the mission school. She was unseen by the missionary for twenty-two years. How could the little thing be expected to remember that one brief message about the loving Father above?

But miracle of miracles, her soul was captured. Then she went home, to face only suffering, betrayal, and deception. At length she was deceived into an unfortunate and miserable marriage. But she slaved in the fields to pay her lazy husband's debts. At last, in agony, she cried aloud to the One of whom she had heard so very, very little.

"Oh God, my husband has deceived me; his brother has deceived me; even my mother has deceived me; but You will not deceive me." Then waiting a little, and looking up and stretching out her arms, she continued, "Yes, they have all deceived me, but I am not offended with You. Whatever You do is good."

Later on, in the house of her hateful heathen brother, she was given "a public affront, unforgivable from an Indian point of view, unforgettable." It was so horrible that "it has no English parallel." Shortly before this an old lukewarm Christian she had met by chance (?) had given her the second sermon in her life, a sort of sentence sermon, saying, "In every least thing He will wonderfully guide you." Could it be possible that she had been "guided to that heartless house with its hateful outrage? As she saw it and felt it again, hot shame scorched her. She had been flouted in her brother's house." But by the Divine Presence Mimosa took heart; she forgave; she slept. She accepted it all from her Father in heaven; "Whatever You do is good."

In a somewhat different connection, Amy Carmichael puts in poetry the way most of us meet our sorrows. The first, the most natural way, to get rid of grief is to try to forget it.

He said, "I will forget the dying faces;

The empty places—

They shall be filled again;

O voices mourning deep within me, cease."

Vain, vain the word; vain, vain:
Not in forgetting lieth peace.

That failing, we try to fill in every twenty-four hours with a ceaseless round of activity.

He said, "I will crowd action upon action,
The strife of faction
Shall stir my spirit to flame;
O tears that drown the fire of manhood, cease."
Vain, vain the word; vain, vain:
Not in endeavour lieth peace.

Or, we attempt the opposite. (Fleshly wisdom is resourceful.) We try withdrawal, quiet, aloofness.

He said, "I will withdraw me and be quiet,
Why meddle in life's riot?
Shut be my door to pain.
Desire, thou dost befool me, thou shalt cease."
Vain, vain the word; vain, vain:
Not in aloofness lieth peace.

The next resort is to say, "I am a victim, but I'll submit to the inevitable"—a kind of sour submission.

He said, "I will submit; I am defeated;
God hath depleted
My life of its rich gain.
O futile murmurings; why will ye not cease?"
Vain, vain the word; vain, vain:
Not in submission lieth peace.

Finally, blessed *finally*, all the mistaken ways of the flesh having failed, self dies, and we learn to say, "I accept the will of my God as good and acceptable and perfect, for loss or for gain."

He said, "I will accept the breaking sorrow
Which God to-morrow
Will to His son explain."
Then did the turmoil deep within him cease.
Not vain the word, not vain;
For in acceptance lieth peace.

In another chapter we shall show how utter yieldedness to God must precede resistance of the devil. Many people become nervous wrecks through holding out against and resisting some providential suffering or sickness. They persist in viewing their suffering as the work of the devil and therefore to be resisted. Poor souls, they know not that, in most all such providences, the way of victory and peace is to accept the difficulty as from the Lord. Certainly if they are His, the trouble must get by Him to get to them. God's way of peace is to accept the difficulty in the spirit of their Master. As Jesus said in an hour of great turmoil, "Shall I not drink the cup which My Father has given Me?" (John 18:11).

Miss Carmichael says: "There is no strength to resist the ravaging lion as he prowls about seeking whom he may devour, unless our own hearts have learned to accept the unexplained in our own lives." We can never do better than to say with the Savior, "Your will be done"—not in any sluggish, sleepy resignation as to the inevitable, but in a positive spirit of cooperation with the Lord, actively willing what He wills to "be done."

For a time we had contact with a circle of dear friends where the phrase, "Your will be done," was never used in prayer for a sick person. They held that healing was in the atonement in the same sense that sin was there. They therefore consistently refused to add in their prayer for the sick, "Your will be done." Was it not the will of God to heal everyone, just as He is unwilling that any should perish? Such praying, of course, leads to a resisting and straining of nerve and mind that can drive one almost to insanity. During a sickness, poor untaught Mimosa (perhaps fortunate for her, for she was not mistaught by the Spirit), experienced that when "relief did not always come at once, peace did." She took it for granted that the Lord could heal, but "in acceptance lieth peace." In her simplicity she said, "And is not peace of more importance?"

We have often wondered how Job could better have triumphed over the devil, had he known all about that great destroyer's existence. When his despairing wife cried, "Curse God and die!" Job replied, "The Lord gave, and the Lord has taken away; blessed be the name of the Lord." Many mistaught saints today would have said, "The Lord gave and Satan has taken away—I am therefore going to resist the devil." But Job went through the very valley of loss—even to the smiting of his body with disease—and came out *without the smell of smoke,* yea, without the smell of self upon him.

"I abhor myself," said the old patriarch. How could he have better foiled the devil than to resign himself completely to the good hand of God? Satan came again and again, but in Job he could find not so much as a toehold. Job would not rebel. The devil was foiled. "We conclude, therefore," says Hudson Taylor, "that Job was *not* mistaken, and that *we* shall not be mistaken if we follow his example in accepting all God's providential dealings as from Himself, and are sure that they will issue in ultimate blessing, because God is God, and therefore, 'all things work together for good to them that love God.'"

Let us then sing with Faber:

> *He always wins who sides with God,*
> *To him no chance is lost;*
> *God's will is sweetest to him when*
> *It triumphs at his cost.*
> *Ill, that He blesses, is our good,*
> *And unblest good is ill;*

And all is right that seems most wrong,

If it be His sweet will.

How easily the great apostle could have argued that it was of the devil for him to be in prison. Surely Nero was of the devil. But Paul never hints that Nero is anything but the jailer. He himself is "Paul, the prisoner of Jesus Christ." And it was under Nero that Paul wrote, "There is no authority except from God." All of which reminds us of Samuel Rutherford, that unique and happy sufferer, who once said, "I go soon to my King's palace at Aberdeen." At Aberdeen he was imprisoned. And from that prison he wrote to a friend, "The Lord is with me, I care not what man can do. No person is provided for better than I am. *My chains are even gilded with gold. No pen, no words; nothing can express the beauty of Christ.*"

What could the devil do, pray tell, with such a yielded soul? Surely he would drop him like a hot coal. Such utter submission to Christ as the "Lord of all," (and therefore of every circumstance) is the surest way, the way all divine, to overcome the enemy.

In order to be more than conqueror in all such things, let me be utterly abandoned to my Master. With my ear fastened to His doorpost let me say, "I love my master. I will not go out free."

Real consecration must be able to abide the testing. Madame Guyon, the triumphant mystic of the Middle Ages, puts it thus:

No man can be wholly the Lord's unless he is wholly consecrated to the Lord; and no man can know whether he is thus wholly consecrated except by *tribulation.* That is the test. To rejoice in God's will, when that will imparts nothing but happiness, is easy even for the natural man. But no one but the renovated man . . . can rejoice in the Divine will when it crosses his path, disappoints his expectations, and overwhelms him with sorrow. Trial therefore, instead of being shunned, should be welcomed as the test—and the only true test—of a true state. Beloved souls, there are consolations which pass away, but true and abiding consolation ye will not find except in entire abandonment, and in that love which loves the Cross. He who does not welcome the Cross does not welcome God.

This last phrase, "He who does not welcome the Cross does not welcome God, " brings us face-to-face with the mystery of the sufferings of Christ. No sooner had Adam rebelled against King El Shaddai and plunged out into the far country of his own self-will than God held up before him the bruised Redeemer as the only remedy for the rebellion, the ruin and the wretchedness of sin. For what is sin but "the erection of self unto the supreme power within us? And self will reign, until a Mightier One occupy the throne it has usurped."

"I was quite willing," said one, "that Jesus Christ should be King, so long as He allowed me to be Prime Minister." But self-will in its very nature—its inexorable law—is self destructive.

"He who will not be sweetly ruled by the divine will," said Bernard of Clairvaux, "is penally governed by himself; and he who casts off the easy yoke and light burden of love, must suffer the intolerable load of self-will."

With the Almighty dethroned and with self enthroned, God had to begin again with a new Adam as the new Head of a new race. The last Adam came to undo the work of the first and to crush the head of the serpent. Did the first Adam exalt himself? The last Adam emptied Himself. Did pride drive God from the heart of the first Adam? Christ chose not the palace of a Solomon but an ordinary stall for the place of His birth, and despised Nazareth for His earthly life.

Was the first Adam tested with a paradise of plenty with no need of denial? The last Adam chose to be tested in all points like unto His brethren: in a wilderness, with the wild beasts, forty days without food before the devil arrived. His whole life was a total self-denial. He had nowhere to lay His head. "Though He was a Son, yet He learned obedience by the things which He suffered" (Hebrews 5:8). Finally, after that thrice repeated cry, "Not My will, but Yours, be done," He embraced the Cross—the logical terminus of His life of utter self-renunciation. But no man took His life from Him.

He was a willing victim, "was willing to be spat upon, willing to be reviled, willing to be classed with criminals, willing to hang in ignominy before a jeering rabble upon the accursed tree" (Huegel). "Behold! The Lamb of God who takes away the sin of the world!" (John 1:29). Did He come to save others? "Himself He cannot [and would not] save" (Mark 15:31). Forsaken by His friends, and derided by His enemies, and under the curse of our disobedience—yea, obedient unto such a death He was *willing*. The last Adam was undoing the willful first.

It is eternally true, then, that "he who does not welcome the Cross does not welcome God."

FIFTEEN

The Cross
and the
Will of God

Submission and suffering are utterly contrary to the flesh. The thing man loves more than anything else in the world is himself. The thing man wants is to have his own way and to enjoy himself. Suffering, therefore, always crosses man where self is alive. There, self refuses and rebels.

Suffering is so unwelcome to the flesh that it demands the total surrender of our wills. This therefore explains how that Christ, although sinless and innocent, learned "obedience by the things which He suffered" (Hebrews 5:8). In order to be a perfect Redeemer from sin and self-will, Christ learned under the severest denial and testing to make the will of God supreme, and to keep it supreme, in the face of shame, in the face of suffering, in the face of death. In His deepest suffering He learned His highest obedience. When Mimosa, who had never learned to read, finally met her sister, Star, at the mission school, she reverently gazed upon her Bible and books and said, "You know Him by *learning*; but I know Him by *suffering*."

The whole evil and wretchedness and ruin of sin is that man turned from God's will to do his own. "The redemption of Christ has no reason, no object, and no possibility of success," wrote Andrew Murray, "except in restoring man *to do God's will*. It was for this Jesus died. He gave up His own will; He gave His life rather than do His own will." When He finally dropped His head in death, there was one thing that the pain and suffering and death had been unable to take away from Him, and that was His love for the will of God. He died in that will. Mind you, *only that remained*. But, thank God, it remained. And "he who does the will of God abides forever." As man Jesus won the reward of eternal life. Praise His eternal Name! The world passes away. Let it pass. He remains.

Has the reader noticed that, when the Savior was here upon earth, He was continually bringing man face-to-face with the impossible? He laid upon men commands which were utterly contrary to the flesh and to human understanding. They were often most unreasonable to the mind, as well as ungrateful to the flesh. How impossible and unreasonable to demand that human nature love its enemies, turn the other cheek, rejoice in suffering, in reproach, in persecution, and on through the whole list of impossibles! And what was all this for but to bring men face-to-face with themselves, with deity, and with their need of His grace to do these very impossibles?

The Savior was striking for the citadel of the will. He would therefore cross that human will, contradict it, and bring the individual to conviction and submission. This was the supreme reason why Christ was continually teaching His own about the Cross. By principle and by precept and by parable Christ taught the Cross.

Somebody has said, "God often touches our best comforts that we may live loose to them. It was the doctrine of Jesus, that if thy right hand offend thee, thou must cut it off; and if thy right eye offend thee, thou must pluck it out; that is, if the most dear, the most useful and tender comforts thou enjoyest, stand in thy soul's way, and interrupt thy obedience to the voice of God, and thy conformity to His holy will revealed in thy soul, thou art engaged, under the penalty of damnation, to part with them."

This quotation may sound harsh—"a hard saying" —but Christ did not utter smooth sayings. Since "God is only our God by a birth of His own divine nature within us," the Lord Jesus sought to contradict "the natural" at every point. The Cross symbolized to a perfection that contradiction. Just as His own Cross was the supreme expression of His own perfect obedience, tried to the utmost, so must Jesus bring each disciple, through an awful process of inner crucifixion, to the end of His own self-will, and bring him to do the will of God. As we have said before, Christ did not come to straighten out the natural, but to "cross" it out.

Take the instance of the man with the withered hand. That hand was useless, limp, helpless. It could grasp nothing. The man could not put that hand to the plow. Yet before the gaze of a critical crowd the Savior commanded the man, "Stretch out your hand" (Matthew 12:13). It was an utterly impossible thing and therefore unreasonable. In order to obey such an impossible and unreasonable command, the man had to come to an end of himself through happy subjection to the will of God in Christ. That subjection to the Lord Jesus, as the object of his obedient faith, brought life and power into that withered hand. He did what he couldn't do.

It is even so with us. The Savior says, "If any man will come after me, let him deny himself, and take up his cross, and follow me." We complain that this is the very thing we are utterly unable to do. But our trouble is not with our inability but with our unwillingness. The command reveals the real root of the trouble. The Cross touches self and reveals the unwillingness. The fact remains, however, that if we are to be filled with the life and power of a divine ability, we must begin at the point of His command to do the impossible.

Your hand is withered so that you cannot hand out a tract? May not your real trouble be that you are ashamed of Christ? Christ commands, "Stretch out your hand." You know your trouble is not in your hand. Through your hand, God seeks to touch your heart. To you, it spells death—death to self. But your Savior accepts no compromise. He says, "Do this and you will live" (Luke 10:28). Do this and you will be surprised at the strength He will pour through your poor withered hand. It may come as a surprise to some that we are just here giving a scriptural New Testament application to the Old Testament principle of law. The phrase, "Do this and you shall live" really means, "This death and you will live." Christ has always been and is, "the end [the object or aim] of the law for righteousness to everyone who believes" (Romans 10:4). But space forbids enlargement upon this theme.

You cannot testify before that person or in that society? The Savior says, "Do this and you shall live." Your poor withered tongue will have to be stretched out in testimony right there. You complain, "I'd rather die than do it." Do both. Do this death and you will live. Dare to go forth, even with your poor withered tongue and "confess with your mouth the Lord Jesus." You will thereby overcome the devil by the word of your testimony. But the best blessing will be that self will die in the process. Satan will lose his hold when self embraces the Cross.

Your foot is lame; you cannot walk in obedience to Christ? You cannot go where He says to go? You complain, "Anywhere but there, Lord." Yet He holds you to it. Self *could* go *other* places; that's the reason you say, "Anywhere but *there.*" Christ must dethrone self. Your impotence in the face of His command is plain disobedience. He crosses your will through your foot. He says, "Stand upon your feet." Another, far more lame than you ever were, was found "walking, leaping, and praising God" (Acts 3:8), after obedience to an impossible command. Your lameness will be cured, when you come under Christ. Call Him not Lord unless you obey His commands. Submit yourself, and say with Paul, "I can do all things through Christ who strengthens me" (Philippians 4:13). You will go forth walking and talking and leaping and singing that the will of God is sweet. The tongue of the dumb shall sing. Aye, more, "Then the lame man shall leap as a deer."

The purpose of the Cross of Christ, as all the Savior's teaching, was to set self aside and to bring our hearts and wills into harmony with God. The whole of redemption is to save man from himself and from his wicked pride and self-exaltation. It is the power of the Cross to work in us the blessed will of God. Huegel says:

> Such a claim does the Cross lay upon our hearts that, though our deepest attachments be violated, and what we love more than anything else in the universe, namely, "self," be crucified, we give our consent. We cry out: "Spare nothing, O God, in me that would keep me from merging my life with thine in an everlasting union of love." Here lies the supreme glory of the Cross, and the reason why it is, as Paul says, "the power of God and the wisdom of God." It disposes us to die to "self." That is why it saves. It gets the consent of our wills that we be detached from ourselves and attached to God. Any other kind of salvation would necessarily be fictitious.

Regardless, therefore, of the conditions or difficulties you face in life, in each one see "a chance to die." For die to yourself you must if you would live unto God. Your wishes have been crossed? Your likes and dislikes disregarded, your wisdom discredited, your sensibilities provoked, your opinions ridiculed? You have been falsely accused and your name has been cast out as evil? Take any or all of these up, as your cross, and see, in each of them, a chance to die to your vainglory and pride. You will learn little by little to be led as a lamb to the slaughter.

Self-will and self-justification and self-defense are indeed your greatest foes. Someone says, "Welcome anything that calls you to your only true position, 'Crucified with Christ'." You will then experience the glorious truth, "Christ lives in me."

The life that He imparts is a crucified life. It is a life centered upon God, fixed upon God, a life lived in the will of God. This Christ-life, mark you, is the life of Him who, on the eve of His passion and death, spoke for the first time in His earthly career of "My peace," "My joy"; and in prayer for His own: "that my joy might be fulfilled in them." Christ's joy in life's darkest hour was in the *will of* His Father.

Someone has well said:

Joy is not gush; joy is simply perfect acquiescence in God's will, because the soul delights itself in God Himself. Christ took God as His God and Father, and that brought Him at last to say, 'I delight to do Thy will,' though the cup was the Cross, in such agony as no man knew. It cost Him blood. *It cost Him blood.* O take the Fatherhood of God in the blessed Son the Saviour, and by the Holy Ghost rejoice, rejoice in the will of God, and in nothing else. Bow down your heads and your hearts before God, and let the will, the blessed will of God, be done.

Great strength of will and complete submission to Christ were wonderfully exhibited by George Fox. He was "stiff as a tree, and as pure as a bell, for we could never bow him." On the other hand, when falsely accused and thrown into a horrible dungeon among criminals and most loathsome conditions, he says, "A filthy, nasty place it was, where men and women were put together in a very uncivil manner. Yet, bad as the place was, the prisoners were all made very loving and subject to me, and some of them were convinced of the Truth." Later in life he said: "I was never in prison that it was not the means of bringing multitudes out of their prisons."

And how practical and contagious is this joy! Thrice happy are those who have it. No man can take it from them. "Therefore let those who suffer according to the will of God commit their souls to Him in doing good, as to a faithful Creator" (1 Peter 4:19). Paul says, "It has been granted on behalf of Christ, not only to believe in Him, but also to suffer for His sake" (Philippians 1:29). How sweet is such a word when it comes right from Christ to the one who suffers for His sake, for righteousness' sake, for the sake of others. Madame Guyon knew this blessedness as she cried:

> What sufferings have I not endured in labouring for the souls of others!—sufferings, however, which have never broken my courage, nor diminished my ardour. When God was pleased to call me to Christ's mission, which is a mission of peace and love to the sinful and the wandering, He taught me that I must be willing to be in some sense a partaker of Christ's sufferings. For this mission, God, who gives strength equal to the trials of the day, prepared me by the CRUCIFIXION OF SELF.

SIXTEEN

The Cross
and
Discipline

Mathilde Wrede was a baroness, the daughter of a provincial governor in Finland—an educated, cultured, and gifted musician. In her teens she was taken by the Cross and became Christ's captive.

She literally spent herself for the prisoners of Finland. In her own home "she lived on the same fare as the prisoners in prison, and they knew it," Dr. Ernest Gordon said. "Such were the contrasts in this life—related by birth to the highest breeding and by choice to the greatest need." Regarding the place of affection she held in the hearts of Finnish prisoners, Gordon said that "idolized" would be a lean word. "One ex-convict invited her to his home and slept on the floor before her door like a dog so that she should not be disturbed in any way."

Regarding her tireless ministry and self-disciplined life, Gordon added:

When, after a night of insomnia, she felt a certain reluctance to take up her daily task, she would say to herself encouragingly, "Today I have again the privilege of being occupied with my Father's business." Then while going down the stairway, she would continue, "O my poor body! How tired you are! We are now going to try again to get a-going. Up to now you have shown yourself obedient and patient when love spurred you to work. I thank you. I know that today you will not leave me in the lurch."

What an emancipation! What a redemption! And what is it to be redeemed, if we be not liberated from the lesser, the lower, the lustful? God help us if Christian victory can make us no better than our bodies' inclinations. Thrice happy are those liberated, light-hearted, carefree souls who can almost teasingly encourage their fatigued frames as could Mathilde Wrede. Such "a merry heart does good, like medicine" (Proverbs 17:22). Has the reader leaned on the flesh, been subject to it, attached? And then it has let you down? It is only that you may find the hidden, secret gold of self-discipline. Seek for her as for hidden treasure.

There are those who may wonder and sigh over such a standard. Perhaps to you it is nebulous and unattainable. It is true that until one has come to an end of all strength and purpose and resolution of the flesh, every attempt to practice such self-discipline will lead us to either fortify ourselves in self-righteousness or to the quagmire of Paul's, "What I will to do, that I do not practice" (Romans 7:15). The flesh must be dealt with first and always at the Cross.

Let us illustrate. After Andrew Murray had spoken earnestly about prayer, he received a letter from a noted and devoted minister, who wrote: "As far as I am concerned, it does not seem to help me to hear too much about the life of prayer, the strenuous exertion, the time and trouble and endless effort it will cost us. These things discourage me. I have time after time put them to the test, and the result has always been sadly disappointing."

Mr. Murray replied: "I think I have never mentioned exertion and struggle, because I am so entirely convinced that our efforts are futile, unless we first learn to abide in Christ by a simple faith."

This minister also added: "The message I need is this: 'See that your relationship to your living Savior is what it ought to be. Live in His presence, rejoice in His love, rest in Him.'"

Mr. Murray assured this minister he was quite right, but that, if his relationship to the living Savior was what it ought to be, it would certainly *make possible a successful life of prayer.* But we cannot live in the flesh and pray in the Spirit. Prayerlessness is symptomatic of a life lived in the flesh, a lack of life in the Spirit. It takes life, the life of the Cross, to replace the death-damp of the flesh. This book is being written for that purpose—that we may have the power and ability, as well as desire, to live and to pray and to preach according to God's blessed will.

Only those who understand a measure of the emancipation of the Cross have any thirst for the subject in hand. But the anointed of the Lord, those chosen for spiritual leadership, can no more escape the sword of self-discipline than the field the plow, or the vine the pruning knife. "Pervading all nature," said Herbert Spencer, "we may see at work a stern *Discipline,* which is a little CRUEL, that it may be very KIND."

There is scarcely a thrill comparable to that of witnessing a disciplined military commander lead his men into the thick of battle. Such a man can lead them where he could never drive them. Those who lead others must themselves be disciplined. It is said that in World War I a well-preserved official "tried to persuade the Arabian leader Feisal (afterward king of Iraq) to undertake the impossible; he said that it would end the war at once if Feisal made his men climb about the precipitous country like goats and tear up the railway" (Amy Carmichael in *Kohila*). As Feisal looked at this fellow's "six feet of comfortable body," he asked him if he had ever tried to "goat himself." Those who would lead the Lord's battalions, whether as Sunday school teacher, preacher, or missionary, must learn to "goat themselves" before they can say with Paul, "You became followers of us and of the Lord."

We perhaps little realize the solicitude of our allied leaders, as they face the almost superhuman task of whipping into shape millions of soft civilian young men. In the early days of the war a noted secular writer said: "In my opinion, democracy will not survive unless it is prepared to impose upon itself a discipline as rigid as that which a dictator fixes on a totalitarian state." Our military men knew that the undisciplined, untrained warrior had little or no chance against the disciplined men of the dictator-controlled countries. Their only hope lay in having sufficient time to develop and harden and train our millions to match the already schooled, the disciplined, the fit. In the mercy of God that time was allowed us. Now and then a leader has lashed out against the enervating philosophies of our modern educational system. One such leading general in World War II, a man whose duty for the past years has been to transform civilians into soldiers, says:

> We've had so-called high standards of living for the past generation—and one-third of our youth are unfit for military service. And many that pass our none-too-high physical standards for entrance into the Army require much time and patience to harden physically—even more time and patience to toughen morally. . . .
>
> The biggest job in the Army is to knock the complacency out of young officers and men, to make them realize that only by dint of their greatest effort, their utmost unselfishness, their infinite pains, and their capacity for self-sacrifice . . . will victory be attained. We must arouse in them the spirit of the offensive.
>
> Do you know what these words really mean? Many of our young people, despite their high school and university educations, don't [realize] until they have been in the army among combat troops for months [their] greatest effort, utmost unselfishness, infinite pains, capacity for self-sacrifice.

It will be one of the greatest fortunes of the war if the discipline of the army can "knock the complacency out of" us and make us realize "greatest effort, utmost unselfishness, infinite pains, capacity for self-sacrifice" for His sake.

Someone says, "What dupes we are of our own desires! Destiny has two ways of crushing us—by refusing our wishes and by fulfilling them. But he who only wills what God wills escapes both catastrophes. All things work together for his good."

It should be said of the hero of the Cross more truly than of Edward Wilson of the Antarctic: "The secret of his influence lay in a self-discipline that was as habitual as most men's habits are, an inner culture of mind and heart and will that gave his life a poise, so that he could not be untrue either to himself or his fellow-men."

Why do we dwell upon discipline? Because it can never be separated from discipleship. The Captain of our salvation lived one lifelong renunciation and self-chosen martyrdom. Little wonder, then, that the supreme symbol for New Testament discipleship is that of good soldiery. The military note is struck everywhere. Paul speaks of running, racing, wrestling, soldiering, fighting. To him, life is continually a conflict, a contest, a struggle. To many, *grace* means to get off easy. But "the day of the grace of God that brings for us the discipline of renunciation" (Arthur Way) *we refuse.* To be "strong in the grace that is in Christ Jesus," Paul says, is to "endure hardness as a good soldier." When Paul wished to sting Timothy, the timid, and challenge him to "stir up the gift of God" (2 Timothy 1:6), he said: "For God has not given us a spirit of timidity, but of power and love and discipline" (v. 7 NASB).

Discipline—what an awful word! To this generation the very thought of it is like the sting of cold rain in the face. But true Christian discipline must be rescued from every false fear. While true discipline will never be easy on the flesh—"no man hath a velvet cross"—its main thought is to render us fit for a hard fight, to produce self-control, to stiffen our renewed wills that they may act according to divine principle. True discipline enables us to choose the hard thing if only it will make us a better soldier for Christ.

In one of Israel's national midnights, Gideon blew a trumpet blast; 32,000 responded. But 22,000 of these, the fearful and faint-hearted, slipped silently home. Only 10,000 remained, a courageous company. But courage is not enough. God has an eye to quality in selecting soldiers. God's men must be girt up. God Himself superintends the final sifting of Gideon's army. It is a simple but remarkable test. The remaining 10,000 are taken down to the water to do the insignificant thing of taking a drink. Of these, 9,700 drink to the full. Facing the foe and the stern reality of battle, they still *desire to feel comfortable.* All their lives they had lived in the realm of their *feelings,* indulgent and indifferent. They could not become soldiers overnight. They had never learned obedience, had not learned to live in their wills. Although naturally courageous, their fleshly indulgence manifested unfitness for the fight of faith. Their feelings made them unfit for the fight.

It is said that during the Boer war, when England was depressed and troubled, the government sent for Lord Roberts, and explaining the dark situation, asked if he would undertake the campaign. His quiet answer was, "Yes." Thinking he did not realize all the perils and problems, the chairman put the question again. Field Marshal Lord Roberts replied: "I have been training for this moment for twenty years." No soldier, whether for the king, or for the King of Kings, is made in a day.

But how different the three hundred who remained of Gideon's troops. They were self-disciplined, self-controlled spirits, eager for a fight, their whole system set on winning the battle. They catch a mouthful of water in the palm of the hand—and they are *away*. Gideon has his army, fit for the fight, self-disciplined as well as courageous. They have courage *plus ordered lives*. They are exposed to overwhelming odds. They have to stand the strain, not only of battle, but also of the ridiculous and the unreasonable. Behold a paltry three hundred with pitchers, and lamps, and rams' horns, against men like grasshoppers for multitude—135,000 of them.

God tests his soldiers in the unconscious moment. Our *reaction* when we are under no outward restraint is the final test of character. And character we must have to stand strain. Christ must have soldiers of true grit, able to stand the weight, the sags, the down thrusts of modern society. "Our Gideon is Christ," says D. M. Panton. "He walks up and down among the churches, *watching us classify ourselves.*" Would we please Him who has chosen us to be good soldiers? Then we must not collapse and crumple up under tests.

We are engaged like Gideon in a midnight struggle. The darkness deepens. Dream not that it is day. The problem of discipline, then, becomes a very practical one and acute. The question is one of "re-action." How do we conduct ourselves amidst the providential? How can preferences and tastes, likes and dislikes, feelings and enjoyments enter into the drill of the soldier? Why dream on, in a "Pearl Harbor" of a fool's paradise? Modern society is just that. The night is dark, but we may not be far from home. And remember that as a Christian soldier "one is forced to travel even at noon as if one were going to battle." Most Christians feel (Oh treacherous feelings!) that we are to be "carried to the skies on flowery beds of ease, while others fight on to win their prize and sail through bloody seas."

When Napoleon addressed his troops in his Piedmont campaign, he said: "You have gained battles without cannon, passed rivers without bridges, performed forced marches without shoes, bivouacked without strong liquors, and often without bread. Thanks for your perseverances! But soldiers, you have done nothing—for there remains much to do."

By Calvary's blood and agony, by the crying need of millions; yea, by all the glories these unreached souls may miss, let us lay aside all pettiness, forget our paltry sacrifices, and cease our criminal negligence. Our Napoleon cries out for the self-disciplined, the sacrificial, the man with a passion that is stronger than death—"for there remains much to do."

SEVENTEEN

The Cross and Daily Discipline

How the world of flesh rebukes and reproaches the church! It endures all manner of privation and peril, runs risks that make us shiver—all to achieve its goal.

In their fight to scale Mount Everest some years ago, a company of daring spirits were so bodily fit that they climbed and lived at an altitude of 27,000 feet. They said that dozens of others could do the same "if only they liked," but they couldn't like. The narrator said that these "have not the spirit." He then said of one of the climbers, "Many excelled him in bodily fitness, but where he excelled was in spirit. His spirit drove his body to the utmost limit. His spirit would not allow him to give up. He must make one last desperate effort."

Then the writer added, "The spirit will drive the body on and the body will respond to the spirit."

These men passed through terrific trials, casualties mounted: a broken leg, a clot on the brain, feet frostbitten to the ankles, pneumonia, and deaths.

My friend, have you ever begun to climb? Have you ever entered the ranks? Have you ever so mastered yourself that through the Spirit you can say to the body, as the trembling soldier said going over the top, "Come on, old body. You would shake worse than that if you knew where I am going to take you." It seems to be supposed, by churches everywhere, that believers, young and old, instead of being recruits to Christ's army, are to be "cradled and coddled, and wheeled in a perambulator to heaven under the caressing smiles of their mother church; whereas as a matter of fact, God no sooner saves a soul than his trumpet-blast calls him to suffer hardship as a good soldier of Jesus Christ" (Panton).

In dealing with the subject of self-discipline, it is difficult to escape being stigmatized by some as an ascetic or monk. The whisper of asceticism frightens the easily frightened. But while Paul was neither ascetic nor monk, he knew that "the flesh with its passions and desires" was his most dangerous enemy.

He said: "Thus I fight: not as one who beats the air. But I discipline my body and bring it into subjection" (1Corinthians 9:26–27). Paul knew his dangers; he never ceased to dread the flesh. He was balanced indeed and was therefore alert. He rejoiced, but always "with trembling."

One of the Christian workers of the Dohnavur Fellowship on vacation once wrote: "There is such a loving thought and care here that I sometimes fear lest the soldier-spirit may be weakened rather than strengthened. Everything is made so easy and so comfortable that I feel more than ever the need of the inner, private discipline which defends the soul against sloth and slackness."

The blood of the martyrs is the seed of the Church. When she ceases to bleed, she ceases to bless. She can thrive through persecution but never through peace and plenty. Christ sends not peace, but a sword. But we have become soft. We have ceased to be soldiers, have ceased to storm forts, have ceased to sacrifice. We want spiritual society, not rugged soldiery. The "soft slipper" stage has taken us. "I've had my day—now the rocking chair has gotten me."

We once held meetings with an old preacher who had been a suffering circuit rider. He could say, "I bear in my body the marks of the Lord Jesus." But an hour after a most delicious meal he continued to pat himself on his stomach saying, "That was a good meal; it makes me feel so good." Poor soul, his sermons were yellow. He scarcely looked into his Bible. He had been a soldier once but he had gone soft, had ceased to "goad" himself.

All of which reminds us again of that word of saintly Robert Murray McCheyne that "if Satan can only make a covetous minister a lover of praise, of pleasure, of good-eating, he has ruined your ministry." But McCheyne has ever been known as a soldier. He knew that the Christian life is a climb, a conflict, and first and always, a war. And our campaign enjoys neither intermission nor discharge.

When the slothful flesh would murmur,
Ease would cast her spell,
Set our face as flint till twilight's
Vesper bell.

On Thy brow we see a thorn-crown,
Blood-drops in Thy track,
O forbid that we should ever
Turn us back.

—Amy Carmichael.

But many of my readers are not missionaries, are not ministers, are not what we call "full-time" workers. How does this apply to them in the daily routine of the home, the business, the school, the factory, and the farm? Here are a few of the ways in which discipline will apply.

It will seem severe to some to cut loose from an unholy affection, a fleshly attachment. Have you had a "crush" on somebody? God hates it. You deny it. Deny self there. That is discipline.

Others suffer from a tongue loose at both ends. Such persons will be forced to keep a strict watch over themselves, and cry continually, "Set a watch, O Lord, before my mouth."

Others will learn to endure under the discipline of some ever-present opposition, an opposition of suspicion, of slander, of being wounded in the house at their friends. Their "daily furnace" is the tongue of man. Such is their inescapable lot. What an opportunity to get the gold of self-discipline!

Others will need to exercise a rigid self-discipline, in order to endure patiently that defeat, that failure, that misunderstanding, that utter discrediting of their best efforts.

Are you providentially located? Learn to be faithful right there. Be content. Do not wish yourself to be somewhere else.

Are you naturally hasty, impetuous, and zealous? We knew one such person who never learned to discipline himself "to be quiet." He became sour, then sick—and dead.

A great mother in Israel said: "There are many women who would not be entirely well for anything in the world. No one would enquire about them."

Many parents will suffer a painful inner crucifixion through learning to discipline their children. Those who have not disciplined themselves—how can they discipline their children? Children are being denied proper and godly discipline today because the parents have not yet learned to hate their "own flesh." Not having laid the Cross on his own flesh, the parent denies the Cross to his child. "He who spares his rod hates his son" (Proverb 13:24).

There are still others who are weak, sensitive, and nervous in body. Amy Carmichael, herself possessed of a weak body, wrote "There will be days when the smallest fret, a jarring noise, bustling people, people who drum on the rail of the bed, or knock it, or drop things, a crooked picture, wrong colors put together, a book upside down, something perversely lost among the bed clothes will be ab-

EMBRACED BY THE CROSS

surdly but intensely irritating; even common good
temper will need to be prayed for then; it will not
come of itself."

What then is discipline? Carmichael also wrote:

When I refuse the easy thing
  for love of my dear Lord,
And when I choose the harder
    thing for love of my dear Lord,
And do not make a fuss or
    speak a single grumbling word,
That is discipline.

When everything seems going
    wrong and yet I will not grouse,
When it is hot, and I am tired
    and yet I will not grouse,
But sing a song and do my work
    in school and in the house,
That is discipline.

When Satan whispers, "Scamp your work,"
    to say to him, "I won't,"
When Satan whispers, "Slack a bit,"
    to say to him, "I won't,"

To rule myself and now to wait
    for others' do and don't,
That is discipline.

To trample on that curious thing
    inside me that says "I,"
To think of others always, never,
    never of that "I,"
To learn to live according to
    my Saviour's word, "Deny,"
That is discipline.

David once prayed regarding his enemies, ever-present and lively, "Do not slay them, lest my people forget." It is said that the Spartans refused to allow the destruction of a neighboring city which had often called forth their armies, saying, "Destroy not the whetstone of our young men." All the difficulties of life are to teach us discipline.

But what shall we say about the lack of church discipline? Trace this lack to its root and it will be found in the soft Christians who refuse to separate themselves from the unholy, who refuse to stand out against sin, who refuse to uncover sin in others.

We never cease to thank God for the homes where the parents recognize the perils and pitfalls and flabbiness of this soft age. With each recurring school year we meet up with such, who pray and sacrifice and send their young people to the Prairie Bible Institute for training. They want to see their young people become soldiers of the Cross. They want them delivered from the dilettantisms of modern schools and education. Such homes rise up before us as we write. From such homes have gone forth in this very generation soldiers of the Cross who are girt, ready, sacrificial, sacrificing all, becoming old early in life, but winning for the Lamb the reward of His sufferings.

We wonder whether the father of Dr. J. Hudson Taylor had the least conception of what his son would accomplish under God. The founder of the China Inland Mission came to know the value of a disciplined life and leadership. He was himself brought up under such a leadership. His father was a great disciplinarian. From the *Growth of a Soul* we quote the following regarding his father:

> Though stern and even quick-tempered at times, the influence James Taylor exerted in the life of his son can hardly be overestimated. He was decidedly a disciplinarian. But without some such element in his early training who can tell whether Hudson would ever have become the man he was, by the grace of God. Do we not suffer in these days from too great a tendency to slackness and easy-going? Even Christian parents seem content if they can keep their children moderately happy and good-tempered. But with James Taylor this was not the point. Life has to be lived. Work must be accomplished. People may be consecrated, gifted, devoted, and yet of very little use, because [they are] undisciplined. He was a man with a supreme sense of duty. The thing that ought to be done was the thing that he put first, always.

Ease, pleasure, self-improvement had to take whatever place they could. He was a man of faith, but faith that went hand in hand with works of the most practical kind. It was not enough for him that his children were happy and amused, well-cared-for and obedient even. They must be doing their duty, getting through their daily tasks, acquiring habits that alone could make them dependable men and women in days to come.

EIGHTEEN

The Cross
and
Fruitfulness

From the Dohnavur Fellowship in India comes this story. Various nurses had tried to interest a certain woman about the Way, but she had never been interested. They were simply talking, she thought, and turned an unconcerned and uncomprehending face upon them till she saw Kohila nursing a sick baby. She said nothing for awhile. Then one day she said to her, "Why do you do it? Why do you work for this baby night and day? What makes you do it?"

"It is nothing in me," said Kohila; "it is the love of my Lord Jesus. It is He who gives me love for this baby."

"I have heard talk about Him," said the woman, "but I thought it was only talk; now I have seen Him, and I know it is not mere talk." She listened and accepted Christ in truth, though she knew what it would cost when she returned home.

Two months after she had returned home, she was dead. That death for her meant the end of what she had known must come—sharp persecution for the sake of her newfound Lord; not peace, but a sword. Before her unconcerned and uncomprehending face, Jesus Christ had been "evidently set forth, crucified" in Kohila.

It is only as we embrace and live the Cross that the world sees the Crucified today. There is a sense in which Christ must be lifted up in flesh and blood before the eyes of the world. Only thus can He still "draw all men."

Lightfoot says that in reminding the Galatians of the gospel he preached, Paul said to them: "I placarded Christ crucified before your eyes." The writer's spiritual father was once falsely held up to the scorn and uncomprehending gaze of younger and untaught men. The lambhood of Christ was so exhibited by this man of God that some observers thought him both stupid and ignorant of the plotting of his foes. After the Lord had justified him, discerning saints said, "Well, before their eyes Jesus Christ has been set forth crucified among them." Those who had observed the injustice and abuse heaped upon the old saint felt drawn afresh to the wounded side of their Redeemer.

Robert Murray McCheyne says, "Men return again and again to the few who have mastered the spiritual secret, whose life has been hid with Christ in God. These are of the old-time religion, hung to the nails of the Cross."

Writing from her place of utmost suffering and exile in northern Siberia, Mary said, "There is a

Godless Society here; one of the members became especially attached to me. She said, 'I cannot understand what sort of a person you are, so many here insult and abuse you, but you love them all.' She caused me much suffering, but I prayed for her.

"Later she asked me whether I could love her," Mary continued. "Somehow I stretched out my hands toward her; we embraced each other, and began to cry. Now we pray together. Her name is Barbara."

A few months later another letter came from Mary telling of Barbara's bold confession before the Godless Society, and for which she was sent to prison:

> Yesterday for the first time I saw our dear Barbara in prison. She looked very thin, pale, and with marks of beatings. The only bright thing about her was her eyes, bright and filled with heavenly peace and even joy. How happy are those who have it! It comes through suffering, hence we must not be afraid of any sufferings or privations. I asked her, through the bars, "Barbara, are you not sorry for what you have done?" "No," she firmly responded, "if they would free me, I would go again and tell my comrades about the marvellous love of Christ. I am very glad that the Lord loves me so much and counts me worthy to suffer for Him" (as quoted in William Newell, *Romans*).

Note that the Lamb of God so indwelt Mary that Barbara caught her first glimpse of the supernatural Savior and was drawn to Him. She could not understand, but she felt that Mary had a spiritual secret. Mary had embraced her cross. There Christ was seen. Mary's love for her enemies was the key which opened Barbara's heart.

Oh, to get men in touch with Christ! We must present Him. We must somehow give Him; not merely preach Him, but present Him. We must be so identified with Him that in a certain sense it may be true: "I who speak to you am He" (John 4:26). And where shall He be seen except in death? The Cross is the supreme attraction. C. M. Clow has said: "The symbol of the Christian church is not a burning bush, nor a dove, nor an open book, nor a halo round a submissive head, nor a crown of splendid honour. It is a Cross."

Jolliness may not reveal Jesus to others. Paul said: "Death is working in us, but life in you" (2 Corinthians 4:12). It never occurred to Paul that a "happified" kind of experience was the supreme attraction. God does need a much happier people, but "much affliction, with joy of the Holy Spirit" (1 Thessalonians 1:6) is infinitely deeper than jolliness and gush.

There is only one way in which you and I can draw souls to Christ. That is by the way of the Cross, the way of sacrifice, the way of death. A Spirit-filled evangelist, much used and much abused, said concerning the secret of his fruitful ministry: "We personified Someone, and that was the attraction. I have not the insufferable conceit to suppose that it was anything in me that drew them. I said to Jesus: 'I will suffer anything if you will give me the keys.' And if I am asked what was the secret of our power, I answer: first, love; second, love; third, love. And if you ask how to get it, I answer: first, by sacrifice; second, by sacrifice; third, by sacrifice."

The principle of the Cross must become our law of life. We must thirst for it as for living water. Let Christ be Lawgiver as well as Lamb. And let sacrifice be the law of our daily lives.

> *O cross that liftest up my head,*
> *I dare not ask to fly from thee;*
> *I lay in dust life's glory dead,*
> *And from the ground there blossoms red*
> *Life that shall endless be.*

Certainly the great trouble with many of our orthodox churches is that they are like great grain containers, full of unplanted wheat that has become musty, moldy, and befouled by the rats of envy and jealousy. If only each little grain had been rent asunder from its fellows, cast into the dark, wet earth, buried out of sight, and left alone to endure disintegration and death, what a harvest we would see!

Gospel groups of Christian young people have been multiplied during recent years. This is a cause for much rejoicing. But therein lies a grave danger. The group spirit, the fleshly attachment, the emotional and the natural—all tend to preserve us from becoming God's isolated "corn of wheat." Joseph, the overcomer, learned to be a king "separate from his brethren"—learned during thirteen long years of isolation, slavery, suspicion and slander. Each Christian must learn to live and walk on his own two feet, go alone to his own funeral, climb his own Mount Moriah. The martyrs found it lonely work, and so shall we.

There is no gain but by a loss;
You cannot save but by a cross.
The grain of wheat, to multiply,
Must fall into the ground and die.

Wherever you ripe fields behold,
Waving to God their sheaves of gold,
Be sure some grain of wheat has died,
Some soul has there been crucified;
Someone has wrestled, wept and prayed,
And fought hell's legions undismayed.

We appeal to those who are sick of the shallows and the shams, sick of doing dead things, "sick unto death" of a fruitless, barren existence. Oh barren soul, hear the word of the Lord: "What you sow is not made alive unless it dies" (1 Corinthians 15:36).

Is the reader trying to live the Christian life? To work for Christ? To bear fruit, etc.? You cannot live until you have died. Death precedes life. "Unless a grain of wheat falls into the ground and dies, it remains alone" (John 12:24).

J. Hudson Taylor, founder of the China Inland Mission, once said: "We know how the Lord Jesus became fruitful—not by bearing His cross merely, but by dying on it. Do we know much fellowship with Him in this? There are not two Christs—an easy-going one for easy-going Christians, and a suffering, toiling one for exceptional believers. There is only one Christ. Are you willing to abide in Him, and thus to bear much fruit?" Death is still the gateway to life, life from the dead, life multiplied, life manifold. Self-oblation is still the law of self-preservation, and "self-preservation is the law of self-destruction." We can never escape the law, inexorable and eternal, that self-sacrifice is the condition of all multiplication of life.

Life everywhere replaces death,
In earth, and sea, and sky;
And that the rose may breathe its breath,
Some living thing must die.

Mrs. Penn-Lewis, whose writings have brought blessing to many, tells of a crisis in her life which came after her deliverance from the dominion of sin. While enjoying her happy, joyous experience, she began to read a volume on the Cross. She says,

As I read the book, I clearly saw the way of the Cross, and all that it would mean. At first I flung the book away, and said, "No, I will not go that path. I shall lose all my GLORY experience." But the next day I picked it up again, and the Lord whispered so gently. "If you want deep life, and unbroken communion, with God, *this is the way.*" I thought, "Shall I? No!" And again I put the book away. The third day I again picked it up. Once more the Lord spoke, "If you want fruit, this is the path. I will not take the conscious joy from you; you may keep it if you like;

but it is either that for yourself, or this and fruit. Which will you have?" And then, by His grace, I said, "I choose the path for fruitfulness," and every bit of conscious experience closed. I walked for a time in such complete darkness—the darkness of faith—that it seemed almost as if God did not exist. And again, by His grace, I said, "Yes, I have only got what I agreed to," and on I went. I did not know what the outcome of this would be, until I went to take some meetings, and then I saw the fruit. . . . From that hour I understood, and knew, intelligently, that it was dying, not doing, that produced spiritual fruit. . . . The secret of a fruitful life is—in brief—to pour out to others and want nothing for yourself: to leave yourself utterly in the hands of God and not care what happens to you.

NINETEEN

The Cross
Day by Day

The facts of Christian experience indicate that most believers wander for some time in the wilderness of Romans 7, in the land of a mixed and divided affection, before they enter into the life of victory in Christ. The great apostle himself reveals the tragic breakdown of his own inner life subsequent to his conversion, when he cries out in an agony of despair, "O wretched man that I am! Who will deliver me from this body of death?" (v. 24). Paul then discusses what he earlier learned (and wrote) in Romans 6:11: "You also, reckon yourselves to be dead indeed to sin, but alive to God in Christ Jesus our Lord."

The apostle Paul had come to see that God's deliverance from the thralldom of a loathsome self-life is not through *resolution*, but through *reckoning* on co-crucifixion with Jesus Christ.

Sooner or later most of us as believers awaken to a sense of our sinful selfhood. We, too, would live for Christ. We hunger and thirst after righteousness, but, alas, how tragically self-will thwarts the flow of the living waters. The stream of our life is mixed and muddy. We fight and pray and struggle. We redouble our resolutions. We see that we must experience an inner crucifixion; that the Cross must be at the heart of our Christian lives. We try to crucify ourselves, but all to no avail. Self cannot, will not, crucify self. In utter self-despair we sign our own death sentence, sinking into our death-union with the Crucified One. We let go and let God, yielding ourselves in total self-surrender. Once and for all we take by faith the position God gives us of death and resurrection with Christ.

Such is the beginning of a life of Christian victory —but it is only a beginning. This death-position once *taken* must then be *learned*. The life of the Crucified must be received moment by moment. There is the Cross once and for all, and there is the "cross daily."

It is a lifelong process. "If any one desires to come after Me, let him deny himself, and take up his cross *daily*, and follow Me" (Luke 9:23; italics added). The early disciples must often have seen the long procession of murderers and criminals on their way to crucifixion, carrying their crosses.

This matter of the Cross once-for-all and the "cross daily" is what Bishop Moule calls an "inexhaustible paradox; on one side, a true and total self-denial, on the other, a daily need of self-crucifixion." We are followers of the Crucified. We must surrender to Him once-for-all. There is also what has been called the *"spread-out-surrender,* a surrender which covers our whole sphere of action and lasts all our days." The Cross-life is not an *attainment,* but a lifelong *attitude.* It is not a goal, but a road. There is no ready-made holiness that we can put on like a suit of clothes. God does not show us everything at once.

Those who have entered into the life of Christian victory will all their lives be making deeper discoveries of the depths of self. The scriptural attitude, then, must ever be: "Not as though I had already attained" (Philippians 3:12 KJV).

In remarking upon the "cross *daily*" Bishop Moule insists that it is:

> without intermission, without holiday; now, today, this hour; and then, tomorrow! And the daily "cross"; a something which is to be the instrument of disgrace and execution. . . . And what will that something be? Just whatever gives occasion of ever deeper test to our self-surrender . . . just whatever exposes to shame and death the old aims, and purposes, and plans, the old spirit of self and its life.

New occasions, fresh tests, difficult circumstances—all bring us up against the question of the will of God, or the will of self. If we are hungry to go on with the Lord; if we have an appetite whetted for reality at any cost, then we will set our faces like a flint Crossward. Each of us will find "his cross" in his daily pathway—waiting at his feet. Providential circumstances bring us up against choices which cross self. These will become the instruments of death to our own wills.

The Bishop of Durham sums up the daily cross as:

> Some small trifle of daily routine; a crossing of personal preference in very little things; accumulation of duties, unexpected interruption, unwelcome distraction. Yesterday these things merely fretted you and, internally at least, "upset" you. Today, on the contrary, you take them up, and stretch your hands out upon them, and let them be the occasion of new disgrace and deeper death for that old self-spirit. You take them up in loving, worshiping acceptance. You carry them to their Calvary in thankful submission. And tomorrow you will do the same.

Many times you have cried, "Anything but *that*, Lord." You have feared it might come upon you. And there it is, staring you in the face. To obey God will now occasion new pain and shame and disgrace. But in the divine wisdom it will apply Calvary more deeply to self. Take it up, therefore, stretch your hands out upon it, and there make a fresh break with self. When Christ shouldered His cross, He went forth to lay down His life. That is what you will do as His follower. He means you to embrace this new test as His instrument of your own undoing. There you unlearn self and learn Christ. That circumstance, when embraced, is your "cross." We must not think of our cross as something compulsory or unavoidable such as misfortune, infirmity, or calamity. Our cross is the voluntary embracing of a path which exposes self to fresh denial, disgrace, and death, and which may actually cost us our life. When we embrace the cross, Golgotha is our goal.

Has some occasion caught the reader in a net of suspicion, slander, and humiliation? Shrink not. Expose yourself to the circumstances of His choice. All things are subject to Christ, and "all things work together for good to those who love God" (Romans 8:28). Take up this circumstance, therefore, as your cross; shoulder it and go forth to lose your life. The "world" knows only how to "take it on the chin." But we take it up, embrace it as our cross, stretch out our hands upon it, and lay down our lives. We thus put on the livery of humiliation worn by Christ.

You may be handicapped in health. It is *the one thing* you cannot get over. Now welcome your weakness, and take it up as the instrument of a new death to old ambition and pride. Paul embraced the "thorn" even though it was "a messenger of Satan to buffet" him. He learned: "When I am weak, then I am strong" (2 Corinthians 12:7, 10).

Have you been utterly misrepresented and your good evil spoken of? The Savior says: "Rejoice in that day and leap for joy!" (Luke 6:23). But, before you can rejoice, you must first stretch forth your hands, and be nailed, as it were, to that very falsehood.

A man of God had embraced the pathway of reproach for Christ, had left a modernistic church, and had gone "outside the camp, bearing His reproach" He was maligned and falsely accused as being a "holier-than-thou" kind of Christian. As he turned away, answering them never a word, the Spirit of glory illuminated this truth: "If you are reproached for the name of Christ, [happy] are you" (1 Peter 4:14). He was happy beyond words.

Thus it is that we learn to *die daily*, "always carrying about in the body the dying of the Lord Jesus, that the life of Jesus also may be manifested in our body" (2 Corinthians 4:10). Our lives must be poured again and again into the mold of the cross— "being conformed to His death" (Philippians 3:10). Madame Guyon, the mystic, cried: "O life, which cannot be lost without so many deaths! O death, which can only be attained by the loss of so many lives!"

In his book, *The Cross of Christ*, F. J. Huegel quotes from the *Sunday School Times* as follows:

> Dr. J. G. Fleming tells how, in the days of the Boxer uprising in China, Boxers captured a mission school, blocked all gates but one, placed a cross before it, and sent in word that anyone who trampled on that cross would go free, but that anyone who stepped around it would be killed. The first seven, we are told, trampled on the cross, and were allowed to go free. The eighth, a girl, knelt before the cross, and was shot. All the rest in a line of a hundred students followed her example.

In order to avoid pain, humiliation, disgrace, and death, we can trample on our cross and go forth to a false freedom; or, we can kneel in worshipful acceptance, and carry it to our Calvary in thankful submission, there to find "the liberty by which Christ has made us free," the "joy inexpressible and full of glory" (Galatians 5:1; 1 Peter 1:8).

And all through life I see a cross,
Where the sons of God yield up their breath;
There is no gain except by loss;
There is no life except by death;
There is no vision but by faith;
No glory but by bearing shame;
No justice but by taking blame;
And that Eternal Passion saith—
Be emptied of glory and might and name.

Has the reader embraced "his cross" today? And tomorrow will you do—the same?

TWENTY

The Cross
and
Attainment

A boy was once seen walking home after the martyr fires had been burning brightly at Smithfield. Someone said to him: "My boy, why were you there?" Like a true follower of the Lamb he replied, "I want to learn the way."

When "Bloody Mary," as she has been called, had forbidden the proclamation of the simple gospel, Lawrence Sanders was constrained to obey God rather than man. When sentenced to death before the Lord Chancellor, Sanders answered: "Welcome be it, whatever the will of God shall be, either life or death; I tell you truly I have *learned to die*." Taking the stake to which he was to be chained and burned, he kissed it saying, "Welcome the Cross of Christ, welcome everlasting life."

Do such martyr stories seem to belong to another world, to another order of life? Shame on us that we think so. If, however, it is our eternal passion to press on to know Christ, we shall soon discover that the crucified Lord must have crucified followers; that as we glory in the Cross for our salvation, so we must embrace the Cross for self-crucifixion. We cannot sever the outward from the inward cross. Shame on me if I think there is a Cross for Jesus but none for me. Let me embrace the way of the Cross and learn to die.

When we first came to Christ, the Cross was our only attraction. By His blood alone could we have been reconciled to God. Later perhaps, we came to see the deeper meaning in His death, that when He died for us we also died with Him. We learned that we have been crucified together with Him, identified with Him in death and resurrection as God's way of victory over sin. Paul says that, having obeyed from the heart that pattern or "form of doctrine to which [we] were delivered" through our vital union with Christ in death and resurrection, we were "set free from [the old mastery of] sin" (Romans 6:17–18). Emancipation came through our having been handed over, or delivered up to, the Cross-form of doctrine.

That truth has gripped us as in a vise—we do belong to our new Master, the Crucified One. But it is just here that many honest believers may begin to fail. Having reckoned themselves "dead indeed unto sin, but alive unto God through Jesus Christ our Lord," they almost unconsciously begin to feel that they have *attained*. They almost feel that for them the Cross is past and done with. They forget that their lifelong fellowship is to be with the Crucified, and that if the Crucified is to abide in them, they must know Him in the fellowship of His sufferings as the daily experience of life. How can we abide daily in the Crucified unless our lives be poured again and again into the form, or mold, of the Cross? The offense of the Cross has not ceased, except in the case of those who have refused to live crucified lives, "All who desire to live godly in Christ Jesus will suffer persecution" (2 Timothy 3:12).

The moment we begin to live Christlike lives, we hear the apostle say, "Let this mind be in you which was also in Christ Jesus" (Philippians 2:5). And what was that mind? When He was in the form of God He emptied Himself; He came in the likeness of men; He took the form of a servant; He humbled Himself; He "became obedient to the point of death, even the death of the cross" (see 2:7–8). Am I a follower of the Lamb? His was a path of self-emptying and learning of obedience by the things which He suffered. The law of the Master must be the law for the disciple.

Charles Simeon, the great Cambridge preacher, was poured again and again into the mold of the Cross. Hear his own sorrowful story (as quoted in A. J. Gordon, *Two-Fold Life*), as he had wrung out to him the bitter dregs of persecution:

I strolled forth one day, buffeted and afflicted, with my little Testament in my hand. I prayed earnestly that, on opening the Book, I might find some text which should sustain me. The first text which caught my eye was this, "They found a man of Cyrene, Simon by name; him they compelled to bear his cross." You know Simon is the same name as Simeon. What a word of instruction was here—what a blessed hint for my encouragement! To have the cross laid upon me, that I might bear it after Jesus—what a privilege! It was enough. Now I could leap and sing for joy, as one whom Jesus was honouring with a participation in His sufferings. And when I read *that* I said, "Lord lay it on me, lay it on me; I will gladly bear the cross for Thy sake." And I henceforth bound persecution as a wreath of glory round my brow!

Such is the pathway and victory, yea, the glory of the Cross. Again, and yet again, we must be brought to the end of ourselves. That is the work of the Cross. At Calvary, Christ laid down His life. We, too, must learn to lose our lives, learn to lay them down gladly for Christ's sake. Let us learn to bind upon our brow, as a wreath of victory, every circumstance of life which brings us to new heart searchings, and humblings, and self-surrender, and the courageous sacrifice of every idol. Let us be bold and deathless, uncompromising and uncomplaining as we embrace our cross daily; and then, let us look unfalteringly unto Jesus crucified to carry us up with Himself into new resurrection power and liberty.

In spite of all that the great apostle of suffering went through from the moment that he met the Crucified Christ on the way to Damascus, Paul cried out at the last of his life, "That I may know Him and the power of His resurrection, and the fellowship of His sufferings, being conformed to *His death*" (Philippians 3:10; italics added). Gordon Watt says, "We do need to be careful not to emphasize a truth out of right proportion; not to preach what I have been calling the death side of the Cross so as to forget the life side of the Cross. That is what many, I fear, are doing today—forgetting that the constant reassertion of the self-life can be dealt with only by the Cross, and that only in the measure in which we enter into the death-union with Christ can we know the resurrection life of Christ."

Most Christians fail to follow Paul into the deepest meaning of the Cross. Paul had long known Christ and "the power of His resurrection." But when we find Paul longing for fuller maturity in the spiritual life—"not that I have already attained"—we find him longing for a still deeper fellowship with Christ in His sufferings. Paul has as his goal, "being conformed to His death." As C. A. Fox has expressed it, "The climax of the risen life gravitates, strange to say, back to the Cross." We fear that many Christians are attempting, through determination and imagination, to seat themselves in the heavenlies without being incorporated more deeply into their death-union with Christ.

"Conformity to His death " will come to be experienced in very practical and commonplace ways. For instance:

- Christ was "crucified through weakness." Am I "weak with him"? Or, do I unconsciously try to skirt the Cross and continue asking for baptisms of power? It is only as "the Crucified" that He pours upon us His Spirit.
- Christ emptied Himself, becoming the poorest of the poor. Should I utterly avoid this likeness to Christ, merely spending upon myself?

- Jesus was made in all things like His brethren. Have I ever been poured into the mold of my brother's misery? Such may be my cross.
- My Lord was set at nought. Has anybody yet set me at zero and found me uncomplaining?
- Christ was willingly classed with criminals. Do I seek the better society?
- Christ made Himself of no reputation. Am I seeking in any way to make one?
- Christ and all the apostles were "made a spectacle (or theater) to the world, both to angels and to men." Do I shun the path of becoming a laughingstock? Do I honestly esteem His reproach greater riches than the smile of the world, even the religious world?
- Jesus went a little farther and fell on His face. Have I certain limits where I say, "Thus far and no farther will I follow the Crucified"?
- Jesus felt the pang and agony and pain of the Cross all His life. Do we glory in the Cross or do we just talk about it and preach about it?

God forgive us for living so unidentified with the Cross that the world can see nothing of Him. For it is only as we embrace our cross that the world can behold the Crucified One. Amy Carmichael asks,

Who would go so far as even to wish to be
Dead to the world and its applause,
To all the customs, fashions, laws,
Of those who hate the humbling Cross?

But how absolutely necessary it is that I be just that—yes, all that—if I would be conformed to His image.

TWENTY-ONE

The Cross, Contentment, and Complacency

We are so likely to fail to relate a little thing like godly contentment to the life of Christian victory. Through complaint, or murmur, or an inward refusal of some providential place or circumstance, we can refuse the Cross. Madame Guyon, whose life of victory has lighted the way for many suffering saints, felt it necessary after a very severe sickness to move a few miles away from the lake where she had been situated. Concerning the only house she could obtain, this lady of French society said:

It had a look of the greatest poverty, and had no chimney except in the kitchen, through which one was obliged to pass to go to the chamber. I gave up the largest chamber to my daughter and the maid. The chamber reserved to myself was a very small one; and I ascended to it by a ladder. Having no furniture of my own except some beds, quite plain and homely, I bought a few cheap chairs, and such articles of earthen and wooden ware as were necessary. I fancied everything better on wood than on plate. Never did I enjoy a greater content than in this hovel. It seemed to me entirely conformable to the littleness and simplicity which characterize the true life in Christ.

She was content. The following letter is from one of our older students who had experienced a wonderful redemption from sin and fast society. She found contentment too. She was struck with a lengthy illness just one year prior to her graduation; she wrote this letter to one of her fellow students from the sanatorium where she rested. It reveals such a deep spiritual insight into the various principles of the Cross that we quote from it at some length:

Today, I have been meditating about "bearing your cross," the "thorn in the flesh," and "suffering shame for His name"—three aspects of the Christian life that are very often confused with one another, I believe. It all came to me this way: Real friends, writing or visiting, have gone sickly sweet at times with such words as, "Oh, you poor, dear girl. Your cross is heavy to bear, etc., etc." Others have said: "Rejoice that you are counted worthy to suffer, dear girl, for His name." It all seems so ridiculous that it makes me disgusted.

I don't count this illness as even a thorn in my flesh, for, if it were a thorn it would have to be grievous, would it not? But it hasn't been. It has been blessed. It is not "bearing my cross" because "taking up the cross" is what Christians are free to choose to do. I didn't exactly choose to come out here, or to be ill, did I? Nor is it suffering for His name, because that would mean I was being persecuted for Christ's sake, and that has no part with my illness, though it has been part of my blessed experience here at times.

Aren't Christian people careless in the way they pick up a biblical phrase and apply it to any and every situation? It is positively irritating at times. The straw that broke the camel's back, so to speak, was a drippy, "sedimental" letter from a good Christian lady the other day. She feels so sorry for me "bearing my hard, cruel cross out here alone." I wanted to shout so loud that she could hear me way up in the city that I wasn't bearing any cross by being ill, and that I wasn't alone either.

That all started me thinking. If we feel a thorn prick, we raise our heads and [accept the] acclaim for a sacrificial spirit; or we heave a sigh and say to ourselves, "my cross is heavy, but I will bear it." But "our cross" is not "a thorn." The cross is different, is it not? It is something far too easily shunned and gotten out from under. But a thorn God gives, and it is not escapable. I think it is health sometimes. Milton's thorn was probably his blindness. I think I will find my inability to do much even after I am dismissed from the sanatorium [to be] my thorn, in that it will be somewhat of a handicap to the work I would do for the Lord. It is probably a thorn to you too, is it not? But we would never think of this handicap as a cross, would we? The cross is indeed obligatory to a Spirit-filled life of discipleship, but it is something *we love*, and rejoice to carry. We embrace it, and the cross becomes sweet to us, making all bitter waters through which we pass sweet also. Suffering shame for His name is extra; it is an added blessing after the cross, I think. Not everyone is counted worthy to suffer shame for His name.

The above letter has been a blessing to many people. This young woman, seriously ill with the sentence of death in herself, so completely embraced her handicap and stretched her hands upon it, and so lost her own love of life, that she became oblivious of any bearing of the cross. The Cross became to her in measure what it was to Samuel Rutherford: "Christ's Cross is the sweetest burden that ever I bare; it is such a burden as wings are to a bird, or sails to a ship, to carry me forward to my harbour."

Lest some of our readers be inclined to think that this young woman had *attained* a degree of spirituality that would insure her success evermore, we sound this warning: The last time we saw her, apparently well, she was living an utterly worldly life. She had failed to keep the Cross between her and that "former manner of life." The Cross embraced once-for-all in full surrender must be followed by the cross daily. We must press forward to know "the fellowship of His sufferings," having as our goal nothing short of "conformity to His death." Be this my life-long attitude!

The reader will pardon the following rather amusing exchanges. They are much to the point in connection with this chapter: A missionary leader was about to send into service a young preacher who had but recently taken the way of shame. A friend of mine wrote to this leader as follows: "Do you not know, have you not considered, that sending Mr. —— out in work before rigor mortis is fully established is snatching a corpse on its way to the grave? Ashes to ashes, dust to dust. No grave, no resurrection: only resuscitation. A crape with no bier to follow."

Later this young preacher, after experiencing some success in his ministry, wrote to the missionary leader saying, "I am sure rigor mortis is fully established." My friend wrote another letter as follows:

"Give Mr. —— my kindest regards and tell him that the corpse is the only one at a funeral that does not know that it (the aforesaid corpse) is a stiff. This rule is invariable. Any archaeologist will tell you that a mummy 5,000 years old does not know it is dead. If a corpse says it is dead, it isn't. You do not need to feel its pulse; it is *talking*."

It is only through our life-union with the Lord Jesus Christ at the Cross, and with the eye fixed upon our death with Him, that we can safely say we are "dead indeed unto sin." The basis is never that of *experience* but of *relationship with Him in His death*. The man who is most vitally and experimentally dead unto sin is not the man who is *consciously dead* (a contradiction in experience as well as in nature), but rather the man who is "alive unto God" i.e., *Christ-conscious*. "To me to live is Christ," said the apostle.

Andrew Murray once said concerning the now fallen angels: "It was when they began to look upon themselves with self-complacency that they were led to disobedience." Beloved, let us go on and press on. The only attainment that is worth a fig is a growing attitude of "conformity to His death."

TWENTY TWO

The Cross
and Satan

The writer has a very warm friend (by correspondence) on the mission field whose experience throws a flood of light upon the subject of this chapter. We think it best to withhold his name and field. He says there was a time when to him the biblical Satan was a joke. Then God in His great mercy permitted an awful trial to come into this man's life. He had been a Christian worker for many years, and had seen some fruit. But when the people he wanted to help poisoned his precious little child, this poor man was devoured as by a thousand demons. Although saved, he was so completely defeated by a double-mindedness, that he could not possibly withstand the foe.

His universe was shattered. With his back to the wall, he fought a losing battle. He had been living in "the natural." He was now called upon to go the second mile, to love his enemies and to be thankful for the things that hurt him worse than death. But he could only cry: "What I will to do, that I do not practice."

"God knows the tears I wept," he said. "A desperate hope that would not die, a secret conviction that my Redeemer would somehow see me out of it all, kept me from utter despair and suicide, which Satan more than once whispered to me. But it was all for my good. God was preparing me for a full-orbed view of Calvary. I remembered that even one of the apostles had to be sifted like wheat by this same cruel monster, before he was in a position to really help his brethren. My spiritual weapons in the face of these demon forces were as a toy pistol before a great battleship.

"Furthermore, to my utter dismay, I found that my own carnality and selfishness had given the ground they held to these monsters of hell. I myself had invited them in. I must get rid of 'self'—that was as clear as the noonday sun. Else there could be no hope of final victory. These powers of darkness (demons are as real to me now as God Himself) which were oppressing me to the point of despair, were standing on the very ground which secret selfishness had conceded to them. How was I to get rid of this self-life, which had so long been standing out against Christ and making a way for the enemy to come in like a flood?

"It was then that God focused all my being upon the Cross of Christ, and opened up to me its wondrous meaning. The moment I took the place which all along God was assigning me, namely, a consent to die with Christ and to consign to my Redeemer's tomb my old life, the old man—[then] a new day dawned." It was then "the hosts of hellish spirits were driven from the field of battle and utterly routed."

In the first place, it is evident from this man's experience that a believer will know little of the devil or his working, will know little of how to face his mighty external enemy until the "civil war" with self has been won. In Ephesians 6 Paul introduces the believer's fight with the enemy "against principalities, against powers, against the rulers of the darkness of this age, against spiritual hosts of wickedness in the heavenly places" (v. 12).

Here is an aggressive warfare against mighty but unseen foes in the heavenlies. Into such a warfare the worldly and the self-centered cannot enter. However, in Ephesians 1 and 3, Paul has prepared the believer for just such a warfare. In Ephesians 1 he shows us our place in the heavenlies seated in Christ far above this present evil world. In Ephesians 3 he shows us how we may be so "strengthened with might through [God's] Spirit in the inner man, that Christ may dwell in [our] hearts through faith" (vv. 16–17). Note the order—we "in Christ" up there; then Christ "in us" down here. When Christ thus supplants self, terminates the civil war, and enables me to say, "I have been crucified with Christ; and it is no longer I who live, but Christ lives in me" (Galatians 2:20), then I am ready to face the foe and, like a Christian soldier, deliver souls "out of the mouth of the lion."

But, to repeat, the believer must first of all be delivered from the world (through being seated with

Christ in the heavenlies, Ephesians 1), and then delivered from the power of the flesh (through an experimental indwelling of Christ in his heart, Ephesians 3) before he is ready to face the devil in open combat. As long as the believer lives for the world or the flesh, small harm he can do the devil. Until he thus becomes Christ's warrior, he is "easy meat" for the devil.

A great Bible teacher, who we fear had gone "soft," was expressing a "syrupy" sympathy for certain preachers who seemed to be so "tormented by the devil," as he put it. After he had so fully expressed this sentiment we could not but say, "But brother, why give place to the devil?" This teacher insisted, however, that all the blame lay at the door of the devil. Since that day we have often been inclined to ask: "Which devil do you mean?" William Law says, "Self is not only the seat and habitation, but the very life of sin; the works of the devil are all wrought in self; it is his peculiar workshop." One of the most subtle forms of self, therefore, is to blame the devil. But why blame the devil when you give him place? His "bridgehead" is plainly the self-life which you allow to exist. Self can never cast out self, much less Satan.

Paul wrote, "Nor give place to the devil" (Ephesians 4:27). Concerning Satan, the Lord Jesus said: "The ruler of this world is coming, and he has nothing in Me"(John 14:30). Christ was sinless and selfless. Satan had no ground in Him. Jesus could therefore say, "Away with you, Satan!" He resisted the devil, and He has told us to do the same. But if self is given any place in the life, the harmony with hell is established. Self must go to the Cross, before Satan can be bruised under our feet.

It is significant that James says, "Therefore submit to God. Resist the devil and he will flee from you" (James 4:7). Note here the divine order. Successful resistance to Satan can come only as one submits utterly to God. As long as self plays a part in the life, resistance to the devil is sheer folly. The devil simply says, "Jesus I know, and Paul I know; but who are you?" (Acts 19:15). God's sure road to successful resistance of the devil is first of all to become "victim-victors." Only as we are first Christ's captives, can we stand with Him in conquest over the devil.

This brings us to consider just how Satan's head was bruised. Is Christ indeed the Lion of the tribe of Judah? Jesus plainly ascribes His victory over the devil to the Cross. His uplifting is the judgment of this world's prince. But how? Was he not crucified through weakness—led as a lamb to the slaughter? Has the reader wondered how such a tragedy can be a triumph?

The author puzzled over this. He accepted it simply because the Bible said it. And that is always sufficient reason. But it seemed so utterly irrational. Did not the murderer and father of lies have all his own way at Calvary? Jesus said: "This is your hour, and the power of darkness." The twelve legions of angels He refused. But why turn Himself over to the devil and his dupes? Let the Almighty manifest His power. Send Satan to his own place. Thus reason raves.

But God's ways are above ours. Victories in the ethical world cannot be weighed in the scales of gross matter. Morals and might are not the same. A poor infidel lawyer asks, "If your God is omnipotent, why does He allow the devil to be loose in the world?" That may sound original and clever—as though ten thousand saints have not puzzled over this Gordian knot. God's ways are past finding out. Satan will yet be bound for a thousand years and then again "loosed" as part of God's "ways." But his destiny is the lake of fire. God might have bound the devil to begin with? But why dwell upon "why"? The devil is a pastmaster with ifs and whys.

Saints have learned to lean upon a God of infinite wisdom. They have found Him such. The Cross has already proved to them, "the power of God and the wisdom of God." For them the Cross has cured sin, and has broken the grip of the devil in their lives. They have found that Satan is servant, that the Savior is Master. Furthermore, they see that even now Satan's victims are being taken from him, right under his nose through Calvary's omnipotent attraction. But how? That is still the question.

Paul says concerning the Cross: "Having disarmed principalities and powers, He made a public spectacle of them, triumphing over them in [the Cross]" (Colossians 2:15).

As we face the mystery of this triumph, it is manifest that sheer force has neither part nor lot in the matter. Let us behold the Lamb as He ascends Golgotha's brow. He will go to the Cross undefended and unresisting in utmost obedience to His Father. In a perfectly selfless humanity, He will meet the enemy in final, awful combat. Let him do his worst. Let him empty his last volley. But the last Adam will continue to love the Lord his God with all His heart and His neighbor as Himself. He will refuse to pity Himself, refuse to come down from the Cross, refuse to save Himself.

When God, with averted face, smites His beloved Son as He bears the woes of the world, even in that dreadful hour Christ will still say, "My God." His was an obedience unto death—even the death of the Cross. His victory carries Him to the throne of the universe. The devil hasn't a leg to stand on. He has photographed himself at Calvary. He is the father of lies. He is the murderer of souls, "coming to steal, to mutilate and destroy." He is a lying, deceiving serpent. Together with "the princes of this world," he has slain the holy, the harmless, the undefiled. Now is the judgment of this world. The prince of this world has been cast out. Christ is victor. He has shaken off the demon forces. He has displayed them as His victims.

"Thus, through the triumph which Christ achieved in His death, the ultimate, absolute judgment of the world, the worldly principle, and its prince, potentially took place. The Cross, as Christ viewed it, represented the last standard, 'the last judgment' before which all moral and spiritual principles will be brought for their final unveiling; and there He was victorious." (Dr. Mabie, quoted by Huegel.)

Let us hasten to believe, and bow down, and share in this mighty triumph over the prince of darkness. Through death our Lord Jesus Christ has destroyed him that had the power of death, and even today delivers them who through fear of death were all their lifetime subject to bondage. What does it matter, then, if God allows the devil to waste our hedge and tear our world into shreds, as he did in the case of Job? The "thus-far-and-no-farther" of the Cross stands between us and the adversary. And as we stand crucified together with Christ, and hidden away in the wounds of the Redeemer, Satan is bruised under our feet. He can find nothing to lay hold on. In that position we may reverently say, "He hath nothing in me."

In contrasting his former ministry with that of the present, F. J. Huegel says, "I look back over the years of missionary endeavor before God had opened my eyes to these facts (concerning the dreadful foes of darkness) and hang my head in shame; but I no longer wonder why they were so sterile. I know. Oh, the meager fruits of those years when I blindly beat the air! Yes, Christ was preached and some few brands were plucked from the burning. But there was lacking a vision of the actual nature of the conflict and the awful nature of the foe. I often wondered why so little of the seed sown bore fruit. I never realized the meaning of the Saviour's words: 'Then cometh the devil, and taketh away the word out of their hearts.' I wondered at the terrible death and stagnation which, in spite of years of preaching, remained unshakeable."

Since those days of crisis, this man of God has witnessed mighty rivers of living water flowing out into the parched places of Mexico. Thousands of soldiers have come to the Lord Jesus Christ. There has been a call to battle. The power of Satan has been manifestly dreadful. But God's truth marches on. "Shall the prey be taken from the mighty . . . ?

But thus says the Lord: 'Even the captives of the mighty shall be taken away, and the prey of the terrible be delivered; for I will contend with him who contends with you" (Isaiah 49:24–25). Realizing this eternal wastage of souls, and how the great Captain of our salvation is so straitened within the narrow confines of our self-centeredness, little wonder that this missionary from Mexico, with his eyes open to see the war on the saints, longs for the church to become as "terrible as an army with banners," liberated from the "swaddling clothes of Christian babyhood."

Surely the lost chord in the Christian church is that of good soldiery. Of all the symbols employed by the great apostle to call the church to activity, this seems to be the uppermost. The Christian must be first and always a soldier. He must cease the civilian life of the worldling. "No one engaged in warfare entangles himself with the affairs of this life" (2 Timothy 2:4). He is forever engaged in an aggressive, relentless and deathless warfare. Only the soft pussyfoot dislikes to hear about Christian warfare. But Paul talked in terms of the military. "His epistles bristle with figures drawn from battle." We make no apology for quoting further from Mr. Huegel. He says,

> How sweet to go on singing about God's love when the Cross is calling to sacrifice and suffering and a bleeding ministry on behalf of dying souls—and how devilish! If there were not so many Christians being rocked in the cradle of the infancy of the faith, content with their own personal salvation, cooing to the sweet lullabies of spiritual babyhood, the world

would not be reeling like a drunkard toward another international deluge. John 14 is your favorite chapter? Have you ever wondered if the devil would not have it so? Why not shake off the swaddling clothes and move on to Romans 6, Matthew 28:18–20, Colossians 1:24 and a host of similar passages that cut like a knife into our silly self-satisfaction.

Oh, the pity of it, the shame, the awful tragedy of it all! Emancipated, redeemed, and blood-bought, but still in bondage to the world, to the flesh, and to the devil. In retreat and defeat, flouted and routed!

Soldiers of Christ, halt! About-face! Claim your freedoms—crucified to *the world,* crucified to *the flesh,* crucified just where *the serpent was crushed.* Three glorious freedoms!

Now we are ready to fight the good fight. "And they overcame him by the blood of the Lamb and by the word of their testimony, and they did not love their lives to the death" (Revelation 12:11). Three all-sufficient weapons!

Having overcome all—Stand!

TWENTY-THREE

The Cross
and
Kingship

His brother had just been poisoned because he was a Christian chief. The pagan tribe, with less than a dozen Christians, had learned by former experiences that Christian chiefs—well, there were none like them.

"Have you considered taking the position as chief of this pagan tribe?" asked the missionary.

"Yes, I have prayed about it and I believe I should accept the position."

"But do you realize all the risk it involves? Your brother was poisoned just because he was a Christian."

"Yes, I know that. I do not know what day I may be poisoned, but what a great opportunity for serving these people!"

Renouncing all that he had, even to life itself, he accepted the position as chief. Jesus said: "Whoever desires to be first among you, let him be your slave"

(Matthew 20:27). Kingship is conditioned upon sacrificial service. It springs from life sacrificed for others.

Homer, the poet, said: "All kings are shepherds of the people." How good! The true Shepherd is indeed a King. And no king is true who is not first a shepherd. His authority to reign is based upon his care for the sheep. His willingness to lay down his life for the sheep is the condition of his kingship.

The first Adam was created to have dominion. He was commissioned a king. In the single prohibition not to eat of the forbidden tree, man was reminded of the limitation of that kingship as properly under the government of God. But man forfeited his regal power. When he dethroned God from his heart and enthroned self, he was "sold under sin." Himself a slave, he has lost his fitness for kingship.

The thing man loves more than anything else is to have his own way. Such is the supremacy of self. Abdicate? Never! And until a Mightier One shall dethrone self and reign supreme, man is an incurably selfish degenerate. Dominated by self, he is up against a dead-end street.

> *Myself, arch-traitor to myself;*
> *My hollowest friend, my deadliest foe,*
> *My clog whatever road I go.*
> *—Christina Rossetti.*

How to reinstate the divine rule? How to free man, the prisoner, from his self-centeredness? How to compel him to sever the tie and make an eternal break with the usurper? In a word, how to dispose man to die to self? The more one grows in the grace of God, the more he learns that mere power and brute force are secondaries with God. "He lifts up the isles as a very little thing," Isaiah writes (40:15). He speaks and worlds are flung out into space. But how achieve an unforced, uncompelled victory over man—one that will "settle sin's accounts," and lead man to an eternal forsaking of his shameful folly and pride? Man must be left free. Where would be the moral glory to the Creator that men should be forced by the sheer weight of the Almighty to believe and submit and obey?

> O loving wisdom of our God
> When all was sin and shame,
> A second Adam to the fight
> And to the rescue came!
> —Newman.

This new Adam came, a new Head of a new race. He "did not come to be served, but to serve, and to give His life a ransom for many" (Matthew 20:28). He came to die, to reconcile the rebel, to decenter man from himself and pivot him again on God. All the way "from the throne of highest glory, to the Cross of deepest woe" He demonstrated how delightful is loving obedience to God. In a perfectly selfless manhood, and by an infinite descent into the depths of a voluntary death, He brought an end to the reign of pride. When He set His face steadfastly

185

to go to Jerusalem, He went forward to the Cross and "took it as it had been a crown." He had come to do His Father's will. That will was death. In that will He died. He died *rather than* sin. He died *for* sin. He died *unto* sin. And such an obedient and victorious life did He forge in Calvary's sacred fires, that now indeed "is the judgment of this world." The "self-life," whether of men, or demons, or devil, is forever condemned.

On the basis of that Cross, God now deals with man—through the persuasion of Christ's death, never that of mere coercion. But if man can still stand at the foot of the Cross without making an ash-heap of his pride—if he will still give place to the devil by refusing to die with his Lord—well, God has no recourse; hope is dead. For all such, the "rod of iron" is heaven's only rule. Every knee to Christ must bow. His enemies will yet lick the dust.

In the meantime, Christ takes captives at the Cross. Calvary eclipses all the power of all the thrones of the world. What earthly power can dethrone self and unseat a man from the throne of every earthly ambition? Christ is King of Kings—from the Cross. An earthly monarch has been known to kill his subject by a look. Christ slaughters man, not by force or terror, but by Himself being slain. He slays man to his pride and every other selfish consideration.

As Huegel notes, never could a "king lay hold of the heart of a subject as the cross lays hold of the life of a saint. And this in the face of a judgment so adverse to the soul's selfish interests that it spells death." All other loves, whether of home, or kindred, of country, or of life itself, may prove but spells that lose their charm, persuasives that lose their power; but in the Cross is that immortal root of a love that is stronger than death.

It is said that when the physicians were probing among the shattered ribs for the fatal bullet, the loyal French soldier said: " A little deeper and you will find the Emperor." In the heart of his being, he loved his king. There are conditions and circumstances, possibly a whole crown of thorns, that probe us deeply these days; but the design of the Cross is to make us "more than conquerors" in all these things. Calvary re-creates kings—kings in Christ—kings amidst all conditions.

Stephen the martyr, ringed in by wolves, reigned a king; every stone on that upturned brow fell upon *the King*. Saul, the killer, got his first glimpse of the crucified Christ mirrored in this man with the angel face. "Who shall separate us from the love of Christ?" When the things of "tribulation, or distress, or persecution, or famine, or nakedness, or peril, or sword" probe into our shattered lives a little deeper than ever before, do they find the king-self unseated and Christ enthroned? Has the Cross so conquered my inner life that Christ is King over all my circumstances?

God has made us kings through the Crucified One, but there can be no kingship while we ourselves are still in chains. "He is not escaped who drags his chain," says an old French proverb.

When the physician was probing into the physical weakness of "Praying Hyde" of India he found that this prayer warrior—a veritable king in the secret place of the Most High—had prayed his heart out of position. An old Calcutta friend says (in the official life of *Praying Hyde*) :

> "We have heard of martyrs who were kept in prison, and in the end were put to death. But have we ever heard of one who was so given up to the ministry of prayer that the strain of a daily burden brought him into a premature grave?"
>
> "No, friend," answers another brother in India, "not a premature grave; it was the grave of Jesus Christ. John Hyde laid down his life calmly and deliberately for the Church of God in India."

Who follows in his train, a kingly crown to gain?

TWENTY-FOUR

The Cross
and
the Crown

Concerning Japan's early persecution of the Ko-
reans, an old missionary said: "Japan could not
have planned better for the Korean Christians if she
had tried." The worst which befalls us often proves
to be the best. It will finally prove to be true, that
the sufferings of the saints in the furnace heated sev-
en times hotter, in the dungeon and concentration
camp, in the Coliseum at the mercy of wild beasts,
before the shooting squad, at the stake, and under
the thumbscrew were actual steps to the throne.

It is said that a Bohemian nobleman was brought
to execution for his Protestant faith. Ere he suffered
under the executioner's ax, the Jesuits made a last
plea.

"No," he said, as he pushed them aside: "I have
finished my course; henceforth there is laid up for
me a crown of righteousness."

The Jesuits rebuffed him: "Those words were true for the apostle, not for you."

"Nay," rejoined the faithful soul; "you forget the rest—'and not to me only, but also to all them that have loved his appearing!'"

As sinners, our call is to salvation. As saints, our call is to suffering. There is the Cross for Christ. And there is also the cross for the believer. In His work of atonement, Christ stands absolutely alone with none to compare. But in a life laid down, Christ is the first, the supreme, the model in a long train of martyrs who have not "loved their lives to the death." Every follower of His has been "born crucified." He is therefore a potential martyr. Christ always associated His sufferings with His glorification. There is no crown without the Cross. Golgotha and glory are forever wedded in the mind of the Savior, so that those who sink into Calvary's depths are assured of the heights of glory. The rewards are sure. Crucifixion with Christ predestines the glory. For there is life, and there is the crown of life; there is righteousness, and the crown of righteousness. It is the difference between being the child of the kingdom and being crowned with reward in the kingdom.

Crowns are for those who have borne their cross. This law is so inflexible that the call to the Cross is truly a call to the crown.

According to the old Latin Vulgate, Psalm 96:10 should read: "Tell it out among the heathen, that the Lord reigneth from the Tree." Justin Martyr accuses the Jews of having deliberately erased the words *a ligno*, lest they establish the rule of the Crucified "from the tree." But to us who are saved, it is from that place of shame and suffering and death that Christ holds sway. To us, the Cross is "the power of God and the wisdom of God." There, the King, the King of the curse—"he who is hanged is accursed of God"—has captured us and fastened us to His chariot wheels. In His utmost weakness and loss, Christ there slaughtered our pride, unseated vain self, and reigns a King. From that throne high and lifted up He holds sway. The "Lion of the tribe of Judah" is the Lamb slain "in the midst of the throne." His reign is from the Tree.

> The truth that David learned to sing,
>
> Its deep fulfilment here attains;
>
> "Tell all the earth the Lord is King!"
>
> Lo, from the Cross, a King He reigns!

The Jews were nonplussed over the apparent contradiction in Old Testament Scripture. They saw there a suffering, dying Messiah. They saw also a ruling, reigning Messiah. Must there be two? They wondered. Of course, the death and resurrection of Christ solve the mystery. Omnipotence has been crowned "from the Tree."

But we repeat, the Cross is not only atoning; it is also exemplary. What is more logical than a crucified Christ so that He may have crucified followers? Head and members must be one. Let us not divorce the doctrine of His Cross from the endurance of our cross. God forbid that we should be "saved by crucifixion and yet saved from crucifixion." The disciple is not above his Lord. Let him then "fill up that which is behind of the afflictions of Christ."

Bishop Pearson once proved the divine origin of Christianity by showing that its doctrines were such that they could not naturally command success.

1. Christianity condemned all other religions.
2. It lays upon men commands contrary to the flesh, viz., the love of enemies and the bearing of the Cross.
3. It makes promises which are seemingly incredible, which cannot be realized or obtained till after this life, and founded on the miracle of resurrection.
4. To seal "the faith" against success, it promised persecutions.

A good argument indeed. However, we are convinced that the Christian faith succeeded, not in spite of these things, but because of them. In the Cross of Christ is displayed the very "wisdom of God" as well as "the power of God." In the Cross is exhibited the whole principle of the Christian faith and life. In Christ's Cross (and in ours as we follow Him), all the seeming beauty of "life under the sun" is stripped away, and we are left with—only God. The world's joys and pleasures are "for a season." The Christian forfeits the present, and chooses to suffer for a season.

A heathen of A.D. 100, Lucian of Samosata said: "The Christians still worship that great man who was crucified. . . . These wretched people have persuaded themselves that they are absolutely deathless, and will live forever, for which reason they think slightly of death, and many willingly surrender themselves." Little wonder that the Cross created such consternation with its inroads into heathenism. The Cross captured men and carried them carefree and happily, yea, even recklessly, through the midst of the most excruciating agonies and tortures and deaths.

These saints became such free citizens of heaven that they could not be subdued to the customs of that sunken society. This contemptible "third race" perplexed the sane (?) among all men. They wore the livery of humiliation and heaven, treated the trifles of time with contempt, and lived the life eternal. To the heathen the doctrine of the Cross seemed, in all its invisible mysterious power, a veritable plague, an infection—once it seized the simpletons! And so it was. In those days the Crucified One was known by His followers. They embraced the Cross so fully because they were so sure of the crown. They took the way of death because it was and is the gateway to life. "Why are you Christians so bent upon death? You are so bent upon death that you make nothing of it." To which the disciple nobly replied: "We are bent, sir, not upon death, but upon life."

We are commanded, "Let this mind be in you which was also in Christ Jesus" (Philippians 2:5), who humbled himself. Thus Christ embodied all He taught. He Himself summarized the principles of all recompense when He said: "Whoever exalts himself will be humbled, and he who humbles himself will be exalted" (Luke 14:11).

From the heights of glory Christ descended, from the Godhead to manhood. As a man, He descended to a servant. From life, He descended to death. From a common death, He descended to that of a criminal. And having plumbed the depths, He is highly exalted or "exalted with all exaltation." His exaltation is measured by His humiliation. His ascent is but His descent reversed. *And ours will be the same.* These fearful facts must so seize upon us that we will begin here and now to shape our lives by this unbreakable law of recompense. Shall we reap what we have never sown? Do we prize seats on the right hand and on the left in the kingdom? God have mercy on any lazy, ambitionless reader who does not care. The Savior rebuked no one for aspiring to the highest. "Earnestly desire the best gifts." We have no option but to choose the very highest. Someone says:

> *God has His best gifts for the few*
> *Who dare to stand the test.*
> *His second choice He has for those*
> *Who will not have His best.*

With the first two lines we agree; with the last two we cannot. He who "picks and chooses," refuses. As we face the Cross, we have no option, no alternative. We must descend to the dust in utmost humiliation. But that *must* is never by coercion. We must choose; we must choose the highest; and the choice must be purely voluntary. We have been destined for a crown only if we choose the Cross. It is for this reason that someone so well says, "If I covet any place on the earth but the dust at the foot of the Cross, then I know nothing of Calvary love."

Is it but a Christmastide sentiment that the Christ of glory was born of a lowly maiden, entered our world in a humble stable, and lived in despised Nazareth? How the devil does becloud these mysteries! Think a moment. Christ was the only one who, before conception, ever chose His mother, chose His place of birth, chose His residence. He left God's glory for one purpose, that He might lay "God's axe at the roots of man's pride." In His very birth He would incarnate all that He would later teach. At every step of His descent, He "made Himself void by His own act" (Moule). Job was stripped involuntarily. Christ stripped Himself. He chose to lay down His life "of Himself." Would He bring many sons unto glory? God's selfless "grain of wheat" fell into the ground and died.

Now note how God began to reverse His descent. From those unplumbed depths of death Christ rose. "Therefore God also has highly exalted Him"—to the very heights of name, and fame, and rank, and rule. And not because of His eternal glories but solely because He humbled Himself as a man. As Gracey notes, from His incarnation, Jesus added "a life that stooped to the lower part of the earth to that which filled the highest heavens. He has thus lifted up our degraded nature, and in Himself crowned it with many crowns. . . . Hence it is, that forevermore Christ's glory must be measured by the depth as well as by the height; for the depth has increased the height." In speaking of the glories of the God-man, the same writer says, "Our humanity rises, rises to the right hand of the eternal throne; but ever amid the burning splendours of that throne is still true humanity."

And he who is joined to the Lord is one spirit. Listen, fellow believer. You and I (let us say it reverently) are blood brothers with the King. He is near of kin. We are "joint-heirs with Christ." He says to you and to me, "My Father and your Father; My God and your God."

The Savior promised: "To him who overcomes I will grant to sit with Me on My throne, as I also overcame and sat down with My Father on His throne" (Revelation 3:21). Joseph was such an overcomer. God's way up for Joseph was down, as it must be for every disciple. His descent was climaxed with false accusation and imprisonment. At every point he suffered for no fault of his own, but solely "for righteousness sake." He had thirteen long years of insult and injury, suspicion and slander, testing and trial and treachery; but all these actually created the king. He said: "God has caused me to be fruitful in the land of my affliction" (Genesis 41:52). And when we see him seated with Pharaoh on his throne, fully forgiving and feeding and caring for his brethren who had sold him, we behold that "boundless unselfishness upon which God confers boundless power." Crowns of righteousness will be conferred upon those who have learned to have the mind which is also in Christ Jesus.

The Savior said: "The meek . . . shall inherit the earth" (Matthew 5:5). Shortly before the American Civil War closed, General Howard had succeeded another officer as head of a special division. General Sherman had been the commanding officer, and when he was arranging for a grand review of the army at Washington, he sent for General Howard.

He told the General that the friends of the other officer insisted upon his riding at the head of the corps. "But it is my command," said Howard, "I am entitled to ride there."

"Of course you are." replied Sherman. "You led the men through Georgia and the Carolinas; but, Howard, you are a Christian and can stand the disappointment."

"If you put it on that ground," said Howard, "there is but one answer. Let him ride at the head of the corps."

"Yes, let him have the honor," said Sherman; "but you will report to me at nine o'clock *and will ride by my side at the head of the army.*" So it is with the Saints who have humbled themselves under the mighty hand of God. The promise is that He will exalt you in due time. Every downward step, every dying to self, every embracing of the Cross—whether in the form of denial or degradation, of suffering or separation, of sorrow or vexation, of false accusation or humiliation—all these and a hundred other things we might mention are not a descent but actually an ascent to the throne. Our call to embrace the Cross is a call to reign with Christ.

Beloved, Christ is coming. He says, "Behold, I am coming quickly, and My reward is with Me, to give every one according to his work" (Revelation 22:12). Crowns of righteousness await all those who love His appearing. Can we respond out of a full heart, "Amen. Even so, come, Lord Jesus"?

"Thy kingdom come." And in our prayers let us ask as never before—for "just enough wood to make a cross."

"Oh Christ, descend! Scarred temple, wear the crown! Bruised hand, take the scepter! Wounded foot, step the throne! Thine is the kingdom!"

Then shall He look us over, the born crucified, not for medals but for our birthmarks, the marks of the Lord Jesus.

Hast thou no scar?
No hidden scar on foot, or side, or hand?
I hear thee sung as mighty in the land,
I hear them hail thy bright ascendant star,
Hast thou no scar?

Hast thou no wound?
Yet I was wounded by the archers, spent,
Leaned Me against a tree to die; and rent
By ravening beasts that compassed me,
*   I swooned:*
Hast thou no wound?

No wound? No scar?
Yet, as the Master shall the servant be,
And pierced are the feet that follow Me;
But thine are whole; can he have followed far
Who has no wound nor scar?
                    —Amy Carmichael.

TWENTY-FIVE

The Cross and Methods

A friend of this author said, "A pioneer, but now retired missionary, to a land where mission work has very largely developed on the 'educate the heathen and hope to win them in the process' plan, [explained] that, in the early days of that work, his mission had discussed the question whether it would preach the gospel despite all hindrances, or whether it would build up schools, and try to win the rising generation and through the students won to Christ seek to evangelize the nation. The latter course was decided upon." Said this man, "I know today, too late, that we failed and, as a result, the gospel has been bound in that land. The other plan would have brought persecution, perhaps even bloodshed; but that would have cleared the air and the gospel would now have been free!"

This account sets before us at once the great fact

that the Cross must be central in our *methods* as well as in our *message*. It is perilously easy to be orthodox as to our message and to deny the Cross in our methods. In our imaginations we would stand again with a hot, dusty missionary at the grave of a fallen hero and say: "Of all the plans ensuring success the most certain is Christ's own—becoming a grain of wheat and falling into the ground and dying." And we would pray afresh as never before: "Lord, give it to us to be so identified with the great Grain of Wheat, that in our very method of presenting Christ, as well as in our message about Christ, we shall set Him forth crucified before the people's eyes."

To the Corinthians, Paul says, "We preach not ourselves, but Christ Jesus the Lord." Tremendous indeed is the task of the preacher and witness for Christ. As an old Scotch theologian said, "No man can bear witness to Christ and to himself at the same time." No man can give at once the impression that he himself is clever and Christ mighty to save. Our supreme task is to press upon men the claims of Christ of a whole-hearted surrender and obedience. To do so, we must create an issue, shut men up to a conclusion. They must face life and death, heaven and hell. Their response must be yes or no—now. We must cut from their feet a kind of no-man's-land neutrality.

The Captain of our salvation prefaced His "Go ye" with His "All power is given unto me in heaven and in earth" (Matthew 28:18–19 KJV). The gospel may seem to have lost this power. The solution lies, however, in our being consciously commissioned by the pierced hand. As ambassadors, we must know our authority. Our gospel has ceased to grip men's souls because we use the language of compromise. The Spirit of Christ can anoint only the utterly uncompromising man. An old soldier once said, "I do not want people who come to me under certain reservations. In battle you want soldiers who fear nothing."

In enumerating his mighty incentives to an unquenchable zeal, the great apostle Paul named two. He said : "Knowing, therefore, the *terror* of the Lord, we persuade men. . . . The *love* of Christ compels us." (2 Corinthians 5:11, 14; italics added). This is the apostolic, the scriptural, the divine order. Paul was moved by *terror* and by a *tearful tenderness* to save perishing men. Today we need this order reestablished. Our preaching is too lovely. It merely scratches the surface of this unafraid generation. In the face of conditions, "as it was in the days of Noah," men have ceased to fear. Noah was "moved with godly fear" to provide an escape for himself and family.

After many years of census-taking in connection with our students of the first year, we have discovered that of all the motives which move people to be saved, "fear" alone claims 60 to 65 percent. Others are moved by desire for peace, joy, rest, deliverance, etc. Between 5 and 10 percent are moved by love. However, this past term we learned that *not one in that class* of over one hundred had been moved by love to be saved. Indeed, 66 percent had been saved through fear. Let all who seek to win souls be instructed from God's Word and from facts rather than from twentieth-century sentiment.

In another connection, Paul refers to "speaking the truth in love." Here is the same divine order. Our first duty is not to speak lovely or to speak in love, but to speak *the truth.* How? "In love." The devil would have us reverse the order. In this same connection we forget that we are *first* to love the Lord our God, before we love our neighbors. If we love our God, we shall then speak the truth to others; and in keeping with the second commandment, we shall speak to them "in love." Let us not offend our God for a supposed love of our neighbors.

It was this glorious compound of a terrible, yet tearful tenderness, that caused the early church to go forth as a terrible army of invaders from another world, bent on taking human hearts captive for their crucified Master. They knew the meaning of Christ's promise: "Because I live, you will also live." They knew the onset of the Spirit. They had "not a spirit of timidity; but of power and love and discipline" (2 Timothy 1:7 NASB). Of *power,* to speak the truth fearlessly; of *love,* that constrained and drove out fear; of *discipline,* that could stand up against all the dreadful engines of torture mustered by the Roman Empire. Oh, the invincibility of such an army! What a presentation of the Crucified! Little wonder they lifted that empire off its hinges, and turned the tide of history. Concerning these invaders, let us repeat what Dr. A. J. Gordon said:

> The help of the world, the patronage of its rulers, the loan of its resources, the use of its methods they utterly refused, lest by employing these they might compromise their king. An invading army main-

tained from an invisible base, and placing more confidence in the leadership of an unseen commander than in all imperial help that might be proffered— that was what so bewildered and angered the heathen, who often desired to make friends with the Christians without abandoning their own gods.

But before we can thus present Christ, there must be many heart searchings and humblings before God. There must be an uncomplaining, uncompromising embracing of the Cross, and an utter and courageous rejection of the idol "self." Ourselves we cannot save.

Some of my readers—let me warn and encourage you—will pass through agonies and inner tortures which will amount to a thousand deaths in order to unlearn the ways and means of the flesh. You may little realize how you lean on your committees on "ways and means." You may be organized to death.

Or, you may have gotten into such habits of ostentation, and swagger, and self-advertising, that it will be like uprooting your very life to allow the Cross to be applied. But, before you can ever lay the Cross on the worldliness in your people, you must first be cut off from all your own "confidence in the flesh."

My heart has been pained over the tragic troubles which bother the average minister. He is "betwixt and between"—of all men most miserable. As somebody put it, "We suffer so much, but so seldom with Christ; we have done so much, and so little will remain; we have known Christ in part, and have so effectively barricaded our hearts against His mighty love, which surely He must yearn to give His disciples above all people." All these things have brought upon many ministers untold frets and worries. Like Saul they are trying to save the kingdom. But they have actually suffered more miseries than the minister who has embraced the Cross.

To *all* ministers I say: The energy of the flesh not only spoils God's work, it spoils your own life and peace.

Your trouble may be that you have been devoted to a cause instead of having the Cross as your sole inspiration, your one and only attraction. You have been ambitious to build your work. But as you contemplate cutting away these fleshly contrivances and false ambitions, you become almost paralyzed with fear. You will be different! You will be reckoned a fool and a fanatic! Oh, the shame you may have to suffer as you humble yourself before your parishioners, your Sunday school, your class! Then think of the contempt you may suffer before your fellow-ministers or fellow-workers. I believe I know how to sympathize with you.

But cheer up. Once you have been undone in the fires of God's furnace, you will come forth without the smell of your religious self. Never again will you be content to live in the smoke of formalism and iciness and stiffness of the flesh. Ah, yes, it will be difficult for God to put His new wine into your old skin. Be earnest, therefore—dead in earnest—but above all things have a holy discontent to offer any longer "dead things, nothings, shams." Let your fears be gone. "Better a thousand times effective peculiarity than ineffective ordinariness" (D. M. Thornton).

Surely our halfhearted and calculating love for the Lord Jesus is the shame of the church, the grief of heaven, and the laughingstock of hell. God cannot stomach the like. He says, "I will vomit you out of My mouth."

But if you persist in remaining unbroken, stouthearted, and self-willed, let me give you the advice of Prof. T. C. Upham, a minister and theologian of a century ago:

> They are slow to learn what is to be done, and equally reluctant to submit to its being done. God desires and intends that they shall be His; but, the hour of their inward redemption not being fully come, they still love the world. They attach their affections first to one object, and then to another. They would, perhaps, be pleased to have God for their portion; but they must have something besides God. In other words, they vainly imagine that they would like to have God and their idols at the same time. And there they remain for a time, fixed, obstinate, inflexible. But God loves them. Therefore, as they will not learn by kindness, they must learn by terror. The sword of Providence and the Spirit is applied successively to every tie that binds them to the world. Their property, their health, their friends, all fall before it. The inward fabric of hopes and joys, where self-love was nourished and pride had its nest, is levelled to the dust. They are smitten within and without . . . to the very extremity of endurance; till they learn, in this dreadful baptism, the inconsistency of the attempted

worship and love of God and Mammon at the same time, and are led to see that God is and ought to be the true and only Sovereign.

It is thus that God chooses His spiritual leaders in the dreadful furnace of affliction. Such leaders can never be made by man nor any combination of men. Neither councils, nor conferences, nor synods, nor schools can make them, but only God.

This process, of course, applies equally to the man in the pew. God knows we should all be spiritual leaders in the vanguard of truth.

To simple, earnest, heart-hungry souls we make our appeal. Seek spiritual liberty as soldiers seek victory in a siege or in a battle. Believe with all your heart that the power of the Spirit will be yours. Sit down and count the cost. Be well assured that the sharp edge of the Cross will be felt, in your own life, and those to whom you witness. We insist that the great lack today is a mighty liberation through an inner crucifixion which will give us holy carefreeness (not fleshiness and lightness—there is far too much of that), so that, without embarrassment, we can witness before small and great, and be instant in season and out of season.

When the whole hierarchy of Jewry gathered themselves together in the first blast of persecution against the Christian church (Acts 4), they were shocked by the boldness of Peter and John. Now spiritual boldness is simply unembarrassed freedom of speech. Where the Spirit of the Lord is, there is liberty. To those fishermen, the Cross was real, vital, fresh. With Christ they were identified, crucified, and liberated.

Theirs was an unembarrassed freedom of speech. Let the hierarchy rave! Christ's captives were free. They would neither fear nor flatter any flesh on the face of the earth. Among these first threatenings the early church fled—but only to her knees. There they prayed, not for the conversion of the hypocrites, nor that they themselves might speak more carefully, more lovingly. They asked nothing for themselves, but only for "all boldness" to present Christ—thereby jeopardizing their lives.

And God was so pleased with such daring and uncompromising spirits that He shook the house where they were assembled. They had ceased to save their own skin. They had no cause to defend. Christ was the living Head of the church. He had died in uttermost weakness; they had died with Him. Be the consequences what they may, they would obey God rather than men. *Neither success nor failure entered into their considerations.* They were not afraid to jostle the Jewish proprieties. They put themselves at heaven's disposal, and when they preached Christ Jesus as Lord, men were "cut to the heart" as the word of the Cross fell like a two-edged sword.

In a generation that glories in the flesh and well nigh worships power, God's choice of weapons seems to be "foolishness" personified. But "the foolishness of God is wiser than men." Indeed, "God has chosen the foolish things of the world to put to shame the things which are mighty; and the base things of the world and the things which are despised God has chosen, and the things which are not, to bring to nothing the things that are, that no flesh should glory in His presence" (1 Corinthians 1:25, 27–29). These are the "things" which Charles Fox called, "God's five-ranked army of decreasing human weakness." Concerning this army, many of us can qualify to enter if we are

> *Foolish* enough to depend on Him for wisdom;
> *Weak* enough to be empowered with His strength;
> *Base* enough to have no honor, but God's honor;
> *Despised* enough to be kept in the dust at His feet;
> *Nothing* enough for God to be everything.

This is a heartening portion for God's people. We are most all among "the poor" who have the gospel preached to them. Paul says, "Not many wise [men] according to the flesh, not many mighty, not many noble, are called" (1:26). God takes the ignoble, the negligible, and the nonentities, things too insignificant even for contempt. Let us then be careful that we despise not our poverty, our stupidity, our insignificance, or even our homeliness. So far from being handicaps, they are all in the direct line of God's choice. Let us, then, seize hold of the opportunity by "yielding our nothingness to God's concealed omnipotence."

The Bible abounds with God's mightiest acts arising from the most trifling causes. God's insignificants—lice, locusts, flies—cause the mighty of Egypt to wail. Think of the little maid who brings life and healing to Naaman, a leader of the Syrian host. A lad armed with only a sling and a stone brings salvation to his people. A cloud no larger than a man's hand causes an abundance of rain to descend. Jericho's walls were blown down by shouts of faith and rams' horns. God incarnate comes as a little Babe, therein lodging and concealing the infinite wisdom and power of God. Five loaves and two fishes feed a multitude. Gideon's three hundred, armed with trumpets and lamps and pitchers, overcome 135,000.

All of this and much more, "that no flesh should glory in His presence" (1:29).

Martin Luther was one of those broken vessels who was fit to bear the lighted Word. He learned that the irresistible might of God lurked in the hidden "word of the Cross." By his fearless proclamation of the truth, he confounded the vainglorious religion of Rome, and set aflame a current of life, and light, and liberty, which has worried every pope until this day. But let us listen to that insignificant monk as he explains the victory of God: "Next to my just cause, it was my mean reputation and mean aspect which gave the Pope his deadly blow; for the Pope thought—'Tis but one poor friar: what can he do against me?'"

In closing this book, let me appeal to every minister, missionary, Sunday school teacher and witness for Christ—and who should not be a witness?—that we sink ourselves afresh into the unplumbed power of the Cross to take the nonentities, the nothings, and the nobodies, and yet make them, even in this infidel and unbelieving age, a mighty host for God.